To

_____

From

_____

Date

_____

CATHY MESSECAR

THE
STAINED GLASS
PICKUP

GLIMPSES OF GOD'S
UNCOMMON WISDOM

LEAFWOOD
PUBLISHERS

The Stained Glass Pickup
Glimpses of God's Uncommon Wisdom

2006 © by Cathy Messecar
All Rights Reserved

ISBN 0-9767790-3-X
Printed in the United States of America

Book design by Greg Jackson, Thinkpen Design

For information:
Leafwood Publishers, Abilene, Texas
1-877-816-4455 toll free
Visit our website:
www.leafwoodpublishers.com

07 08 09 10 11 / 7 6 5 4 3 2

To David—

who still asks me out for Saturday night dates.

Acknowledgements

Love and thanks to: Kenneth and Sylvia Turner, dad and mom, who introduced me to Jesus; my church family who first encouraged my writing; and my children Russell Messecar and Sheryle Bazan. Other supportive friends include Doris Allen, Pat Schuler and Patricia McFarlane. To Jan Tickner, Dr. Donn Taylor, Don Dilmore, and Bob Wilson, my appreciation for your friendship and critiques at Jan's dining table. To *The Courier* newspaper city editor Andy Dubois and news editor Bob Borders, thank you for sharing your publishing expertise. To Dr. Leonard Allen, managing editor of Leafwood Publishers/ACU Press, I truly value your generous spirit in support of this project.

CATHY MESSECAR

Table of Contents

CHAPTER 1

IN THE NAME OF JESUS PRAYING IN A GARDEN

THE STAINED GLASS PICKUP

These commandments...are to be on your hearts. Impress them on your children. Talk about them when you sit at home and when you walk along the roads, when you lie down and when you get up.

DEUTERONOMY 6:6-7

In my line of view, the rugged-looking outdoorsman laid a carefully tended western hat on the pew beside him. He was one of a crowd gathered in an Abilene chapel to hear a speaker, but something about this middle-aged man stirred my spirit, caught my attention. Perhaps it was just the surroundings.

Stained glass paneled the chapel walls from floor to ceiling. The God-made sun shining through the man-made glass created a setting for contemplation and worship of God's holiness.

Teaching about the destruction of Nadab and Abihu, the speaker explained how Aaron's sons had offered sacrifices improperly (Leviticus 10). After their deaths, Aaron also failed to follow God's divine pattern for offering sacrifices; however, he was not destroyed.

The speaker warned against touching God's holiness by making judgments based only on what is seen. He gave proofs that God alone is able to look at an individual's heart and factor in every intent and history of a life. By the end of the lecture, I saw the rancher-type man pick up his hat, hold it in his lap and rub the brim with his fingers.

During a question and answer session the same man spoke up. He mentioned his desire to revere God then asked about one of his prayer

habits. Because time spent with his daughter was limited by his work
schedule, he made it his priority to drive her to high school. While on their
way in his pickup truck, he prayed aloud and asked blessings on her day.

Concerned about giving God divided attention while driving, this dad
didn't want to be too casual with his Holy Father. The speaker assured him
God's concern was his heart, not body posturing or the closing of his eyes.

After hearing the speaker and questioner's exchange, I thought, surely
this shared-worship in the truck cab with his daughter will outweigh the
deed of the ranch he may give her someday.

My husband and I are now parents of adult children, and as we age, we find
our prayer time increasing for our son and daughter. We trust the Receiver
of these prayers to give them spiritual inheritances along their journey.

I'm thankful for the cowboy's example, for the denim-clad dad who
prayed in his pickup, his stained-glass pickup.

FATHER, THANK YOU FOR PRECIOUS MINUTES WITH MY
CHILDREN NO MATTER THEIR AGES, NO MATTER WHERE.
IN THE NAME OF YOUR SON JESUS, BESIDE YOUR THRONE,
WHO STILL INTERCEDES FOR ME.
AMEN.

IN JESUS' NAME

I tell you the truth, my Father will give you whatever you ask in my name.

JOHN 16:23

A new prayer-priority emerged for me: To consciously remember my High Priest Jesus interceding throughout the day. After reading Ruth Gibson's *Chipped Dishes, Zippers & Prayer*, short meditations about marriage, children, neighborhood, and church family, I longed to be aware and give thanksgiving for the different ways Jesus helped me each day.

When Ms. Gibson's children were young she had a difficult decision to make. She wanted to return to graduate school, and she closed her prayer for guidance, "In memory of Jesus, whose mother never went to college."

Ms. Gibson's prayers prompted soul-searching for me. The typical closing phrase after my prayers was "In Jesus' name." Over the years, those final words became a habitual prayer component. Instead of acknowledging the way Jesus life-supported me on any given day, I merely repeated a phrase heard since childhood.

To recognize the hand of the Savior in my daily life became very important to me. Paul understood the abiding presence of Jesus and wrote about the spiritual boosts he received: " . . . I labor, struggling with all his energy, which so powerfully works in me" (Colossians 1:29).

I began to notice that on some days Jesus became my Prince of Peace. On others he revealed himself as Counselor. And one particular night, he crossed stormy seas to climb into my rocking boat.

Nave's Topical Bible lists over 200 names and titles for Jesus. Here are a

few: Servant of Rulers, Faithful and True Witness, Good Master, Finisher
of faith, Captain of the Lord's Host, Righteous Judge, Sanctuary, Vine,
Door, Fountain, Arm of the Lord and a Friend of Sinners.

The Hebrew writer's instructions to "fix your thoughts on Jesus," and
"consider him" became a daily goal. After a time, for I'm a slow-learner,
I began to recognize Jesus' care to be constant, conformed to my needs
and energizing.

Ruth Gibson was a link in bringing me to a deeper relationship with my
Savior. One day, I spoke with her and expressed my thanks because her
written prayers led me to holy ground.

> FATHER, YOU SPOKE TO MOSES, JOSHUA AND THE PRIESTS
> ABOUT HOLY PLACES. NOW I'M REMEMBERING THE BAREFOOT
> CHRIST AND HIS SACRIFICE FOR ME. PLEASE, FORGIVE
> THE CARELESS TIMES I'VE TAGGED THE NAME OF JESUS
> AT THE END OF MY PRAYERS. I ASK IN THE NAME OF THE
> SEVENTY-TIMES-SEVEN FORGIVING SAVIOR.
> AMEN.

SLAYING DRAGONS

The great dragon was hurled down—that ancient serpent called the devil
or Satan, who leads the whole world astray.

REVELATION 12:9

Rubber boots on and lunch pail in hand, my son left for work. After a goodbye kiss he trotted toward his tricycle. My four-year-old son Russell pretended to go to work, like his daddy. I went back inside my home, but within ten seconds the back door flew open, and Russell's ashen face appeared.

"A snake, a snake!" he shouted. Following his point, I saw a water moccasin coiled by our whitewashed gate. I had a shovel handy and slew the reptile, but my son's fear of snakes intensified that day.

Several years later when Russell was eleven, he gave me a handmade card. The front declared "HAPPY MAMA'S DAY." He penned this message inside: "Dear Mom, Thank You For Killing The Snake When I Was Four Years Old! Happy Mother's Day." In the lower left corner he drew a huge star and labeled me a "GOLD STAR SPORT."

My children are adults now, but keeping after their Enemy, "that ancient serpent called the devil," continues to be my lifetime calling. When they were toddlers, I got up in the middle of cold nights and tiptoed into their rooms to pray and make a blanket check. During the teenage years, I quietly went into their rooms to pray as they slept. Often, when they were away from home, elementary school to college, I went into their rooms, sat on their beds and prayed for my son and daughter.

Blanketing these adult children with prayer is now a priority. Even if

I'm miles away physically or in our relationship, I can still touch their worlds and influence the chapters in their new families. Petitions from moms, dads and grandparents prompt God to move obstacles, draw road maps or instill peace.

On my grandmother's very last visit to my mom's house, their physical roles reversed. One evening, Mom helped Grandma put on her nightclothes. Then Dad lifted my wheelchair-bound grandmother onto the bed. Afterward Mom fussed over her, smoothed the bedding and kissed her good night.

A little later when Mom walked through the dark hallway, she heard Grandmother speaking softly. Mom peeked in to see if she was okay and found Grandmother wasn't talking to herself. She was speaking to her Father, praying for her adult children by name. Feeble in body, but strong with a mother's spirit, she was slaying dragons.

FATHER, CALL MAJESTIC FORCES TO SURROUND MY CHILDREN AND GRANDCHILDREN. THANK YOU FOR THE PROTECTIVE BARRIER OF SON AND SPIRIT. IN THE NAME OF JESUS WHO BRUISED THE SERPENT'S HEEL.

AMEN.

MOUNTAINS AND MULBERRIES

*If you have faith as small as a mustard seed, you can say
to this mulberry tree, "Be uprooted and planted in the sea,"
and it will obey you.*

LUKE 17:6

The Master of Prayer encouraged small-faith disciples to go lumber-jacking after big targets. Mountains and mulberries seem not to have much in common, but Jesus used both examples when he taught believers that a command in his name would force even fruit trees and mountains to take flying leaps.

Was Jesus teaching a lesson about physical displacement? Was he assuring his listeners that hard-core mountains are conquerable? Did their stubborn toehold in the earth have a correlation to his lesson? In this teaching-moment, Jesus emphasizes always turning to God.

Jesus inspired his followers to expect results from bringing flecks of faith to God's creative palm. When confronted with his teaching, I ask myself: When did I last ask for something totally believing he would answer? When have I boldly asked for something earthshaking, beyond my imagination?

Hindrances to my prayers happen daily, and I am the biggest stumbling block. One downfall to my prayer life is focusing only on what my physical eyes see. I see the size of my credit card debt. I see the effects of cancer in Lizzie. I see Jerry held captive in a debilitating sin. Physical sight blocks Son-sight.

Another way I hinder prayer is by presenting God with solutions from my imagination. I dream up ways for him to "work" things out. That's when a leafy tree reminds me of Jesus' words.

A mulberry tree stands guard outside my breakfast-room window. In the spring, the tree is a flurry of feathers. As the berries ripen, I watch crows forage and blue jays dart in for fast food. On the windowsill, I prop up an index card that reminds me of Jesus' challenge-words, "You can say to this mulberry tree, 'Be uprooted.'"

In his teachings, Jesus drew bold word-pictures for his followers. His disciples heard and watched as he gave imperative commands and water and wind obeyed. There's never been a reason for me to say to my fruit tree, "Get out of my yard! Go! Plant yourself in the Gulf of Mexico." But through Jesus' examples, I've learned that my faith-seeds can be mega-sized in the hand of God.

The next time I see a clump of hills, I will remember they could hike up their grassy skirts, yank up roots and walk off. I will remember my mulberry tree could wiggle out of the soil and settle in salt water.

I will remember.

FATHER, I STILL STRUGGLE WITH FEEBLE FAITH, BUT I THANK YOU
FOR HEARING MY TIMID VOICE AND WORKING WONDERS TO
YOUR GLORY. I LIFT MY EYES TO THE HILLS AND THANK YOU FOR
THE VISUAL AID SON OF MAN. IN HIS NAME.
AMEN.

CATHY MESSECAR

CHAPTER 2

IN THE NAME OF JESUS
READING FROM THE ISAIAH SCROLL

LAPPING THE BIBLE

Your statutes are wonderful; therefore I obey them. The entrance of your words give light; it gives understanding to the simple. I open my mouth and pant, longing for your commands.

PSALM 119:129-131

On a Sunday in April, my husband and I take an annual trip to see the bluebonnets in Southeast Texas. Arising early, we drive 50 miles and stop at a German bakery for pastries and coffee, and then we worship with a local church. After several years of this routine, the Christians expect to see us during bluebonnet season.

We've noticed a characteristic of their assembled congregation: nearly everyone carries a Bible when they gather to worship, and they use their Bibles to look up key verses referred to in the sermon. Like a classroom during an open-book test, their Bible pages rustle.

Carrying Bibles to church is a good habit. The presence of many Bibles may witness to visitors. Guests have occasion to observe the importance of holy text to a congregation when believers thumb through gilt-worn Bibles.

Members carrying Bibles to worship have opportunities to increase their knowledge. Listening to Christians' comments and running references is good hands-on experience. "Iron sharpens iron, so one man sharpens another" (Proverbs 27:17). In my Bible margins, I've recorded profound wisdom from scholars, friends and children. Names, dates, times and places have also been preserved there.

Even in a crowd, personal biblical understanding may take place.

Scribbled in the white spaces of my Bible are prayers, pleas and confessions. A few misspelled "hallelujahs" are beside verses that swept me away from my way of thinking and closer to God's thoughts. Question marks speckle the pages. Highlighted and annotated passages have become a map of my spiritual journey.

Another benefit of open Bibles in church is that the children learn to imitate adults. Each of my children owned a Bible at a very young age. Before we left for church, I did a quick visual scan of their bodies and extremities—for gum in their hair, slogan T-shirts or stowaway frogs. As we rushed out the door, how many times did I neglect to check to see if their Bibles were in their hands?

The Bible is not to be esteemed above the Savior, but the tome needs a special place in my life. My lap is reserved for special pets, works projects, reading material, a child, or a plate of food, and there's another item I often hold close. I hope the children around me will know The Book is highly valued because they see me "lap" the Bible.

DEAREST GOD, THANK YOU FOR COPIES OF THE BIBLE, LEATHER-
BOUND TO PAPERBACK. PLEASE PUT A COPY IN SEEKERS' HANDS.
I COME THROUGH JESUS WHO READ AND FULFILLED THE WORDS
OF ISAIAH ON A SABBATH IN SYNAGOGUE.
AMEN.

JOB SPOKE TO ME

But what was sown on good soil is the man who hears
the word and understands it. He produces a crop, yielding
a hundred, sixty or thirty times what was sown.

MATTHEW 13:23

About once a month my husband David and I take a trip to New Mexico. No. We don't go skiing, mountain climbing or to a cottage tucked among oil wells. We travel in an eighteen-wheeler and purchase a load of alfalfa hay. The trip is pleasant for several reasons. He gets a change of scenery from his local business, and we get to spend uninterrupted hours with each other. We catch up on our talking because we leave the cellular phone off most of the time.

At a family-owned motel, the proprietor always gives us the same room, and when we arrive in December, the generous owner tells us a man in a red suit and white beard paid for our room. We've made friends with many of the local people over the past twenty years. All around it's a pleasant trip.

On one such trip, our flatbed trailer was being loaded at an old wooden red barn with huge double doors at each end. On the inside, hay was stacked to the rafters on both sides, leaving a path in the middle for trucks.

My husband has various jobs to ready the trailer for the trip home. Two other men stacked and tarped the 700-plus bales in about three hours. I had free time to daydream, take a nap, read or walk.

I found a stray bale of hay in an inconspicuous spot and opened my

Bible to read Daniel. Sometimes at home, my Bible reading, my daily bread, gets shoved to the bottom of my schedule. Bullies such as extra phone calls, chores and fatigue stomp around in my life, discouraging any feeble attempts for quiet time. When I don't make time for breaking a loaf with God, the results are malnutrition of my spirit.

I read several chapters of Daniel before my husband joined me to chat and snack on fat-free caramel popcorn. After he left to adjust chains and move tarps, I continued my popcorn feast, even though not really hungry. Distracted and munching away, I forgot my reading.

A sudden wind came up. A breeze funneled through the barn and fluttered the pages of the Bible on my lap. The gusty wind flipped them open to Job 23. Glancing down, I re-read the only underlined verse.
The words startled me. I closed the foil-bagged corn snacks and began my study of Daniel again. Job's ancient words traversed time and challenged me: "I have treasured the words of His mouth more than my daily bread."

LORD GOD, HELP ME LISTEN TO MY SOUL'S YEARNINGS FOR YOU.
MAY I RESPOND AS READILY TO THOSE DESIRES AS I REACT
WHEN MY STOMACH GROWLS. IN THE NAME OF JESUS
WHO STILL FEEDS MILLIONS TODAY.
AMEN.

BIBLE SNACKS

I run in the path of your commands for you have set my heart free.

PSALM 119:32

Reading my Bible, I often discover a phrase or principle that my heart latches onto. I call those quick insights "Bible snacks." They are easy to remember, store in my heart and retrieve when I need an energy boost from above. Here are two of my favorites.

The first comes from a vision to Zechariah, who saw the Lord Almighty interacting with an angel-messenger. He describes part of his vision, "So the LORD spoke kind and comforting words to the angel who talked with me" (Zechariah1:13).

When I read those words, happiness sprang up like artesian water. To know that God spoke "kind and comforting words" to his angels punctured any gloom in my heart. The thought never crossed my mind that angels might need God's comfort, although they do have quite a job description, ministering and serving today's Christians (Hebrews 1:14).

How angels interact and support Christians is more mystery than knowledge to me, but I'm happy to have all the contented-angel help I can get, for there were a few days when life kicked me and she had on steel-toed boots.

The second "Bible snack" is from the Psalms. David too had his share of troubles, from outside forces and self-infliction, but he still penned these words: "LORD, you have assigned me my portion and my cup; you have made my lot secure. The boundary lines have fallen for me in pleasant places; surely I have a delightful inheritance" (Psalm 16:6).

King David used a surveyor's term to illustrate the borders of his life that fell in "pleasant places." When land is surveyed, often the final boundary markers include a picturesque hill, creek, or mossy oak. But David's thanksgiving extended beyond physical land and his kingship. He applauded his place in God's plan and God's love. I see that his phrasing is a fitting description of my "half-acre" and inheritance in Christ.

God provided a banquet Bible. On some days I get an all-you-can-absorb buffet. Much to my regret, on other days I run through for fast food. However long or short my meal at God's table, he generously allows me to tuck away wisdom-words to reflect on throughout the remainder of the day.

LORD OF LANGUAGES, LORD OF COMFORTING WORDS, THANK YOU FOR THE CINEMATIC PICTURE OF YOU FROM GENESIS TO REVELATION. PLEASE STEP INTO MY OVERCROWDED LIFE AND ARRANGE INTIMATE MOMENTS IN YOUR DINING ROOM. IN THE NAME OF THE CHRIST WHO ROSE EARLY TO SEEK YOU.
AMEN.

STAKING CLAIMS TO PROMISES

Your promises have been thoroughly tested, and your servant loves them.

PSALM 119:140

Yukon and gold-mining claims are still available, and visionaries are planning the process for staking claims on other planets. I'm not really interested in finding a new home for my feet, but I often need a better place to anchor my heart.

In the Bible, I nailed down corner posts and staked my claim to a few promises. Even if they weren't a generic promise, but fit my circumstances, I asked God for similar results. One of my favorite promises is in the Psalms.

David said, "When I called, you answered me; you made me bold and stouthearted" (Psalm 138:3). When I am frail in spirit, I say, "Father, remember when you gave your servant David courage to face wild animals and out-of-control people? Lions are still stalking. Will you make my portion of boldness a large helping?"

David fought against a bear. He slew a lion, and he outsmarted his enemies. When I need and request courage, God also rewards me with an intrepid spirit.

At other times when I need help, I repeat the actions of Bible heroes. One example I follow is King Hezekiah's. While he and his citizens hid inside the walls of Jerusalem, a courier brought a threatening letter from an invading enemy. Judah's king went into the temple, knelt down, and spread the letter before God. In the letter the foreign king ridiculed God.

Hezekiah's specific request was, "Now, O LORD our God, deliver us from his hand, so that all kingdoms on earth may know that you alone, O LORD, are God" (2 Kings 19:19).

God responded by rescuing the city, and the enemies bolted away. Notice of impending difficulty may arrive in paper form as a letter, a debt or summons. When trouble rings my doorbell, I often repeat the actions of Hezekiah, a kneeling king.

Like the earliest Christians, I sometimes catch myself singing in a dark hour. When Paul and Silas were imprisoned, their cellmates might have expected them to hover in a dark corner and lick their wounds. No pity party for them. The two men asked a third party to join them, and Jesus entered their dungeon.

To escape my prison of despair, I sing praise songs alone or with a CD chorus. My voice may have little impact on my world, but a King will receive my songs of praise.

The decisive deeds and requests of long-ago servants are worthy of repetition. I want to follow their lead and stake a claim.

FATHER, THANK YOU FOR THE PRINTED PRAYERS AND CONDUCT OF YOUR TRAILBLAZERS. FOR YOUR LOVING RESPONSE THEN AND NOW, I THANK YOU. THROUGH JESUS, WHO PIONEERED THE WAY TO HEAVEN.

AMEN.

CHAPTER 3

IN THE NAME OF JESUS BRINGING REAL CHARACTER TO THE FAMILY TREE

NEST NEAR HIS ALTAR

Even the sparrow has found a home, and the swallow a nest for herself,
where she may have her young—a place near your altar, O LORD
Almighty, my King and my God. Blessed are those who dwell in your
house; they are ever praising you.

PSALM 84:3-4

Spring arrived and brought a cacophony of twitterings and chirps. In the lower branches of a lemony-smelling magnolia tree a bird's nest took shape. A wren couple brought twigs and pine straw to a galvanized pail hanging on our back porch. Always hungry and pleading at my naptime, a noisy cardinal brood grew to maturity in the yew tree near my bedroom.

Nesting birds instinctively search for a sheltered, safe haven for their young. Our family also found two other unusual nesting sites. One was in the exhaust stack of our out-of-service truck, a '65 B-Model Mack. The other was a deer stand full of baby buzzards.

The Canada goose shows special determination during nesting season. When she plucks soft down from her breast to line her nest, a small bare spot appears, called an incubation patch. As each egg is laid, the mother tucks additional down around the fragile-shelled life before warming her clutch through the patch of bare skin.

These northern geese are known to freeze to death during inclement weather. Despite high winds, they scrunch over and cling to their nests, protecting delicate life.

On calm or stormy days, a great deal of comfort comes from knowing

God is the original bird watcher. Jesus asked his students a rhetorical question to focus their attention toward God's care for sparrows and humans. "Are not two sparrows sold for a penny? Yet not one of them will fall to the ground apart from the will of your Father . . .. So don't be afraid; you are worth more than many sparrows" (Matthew 10:29).

Spring storms, you may howl. Blow and hurl your rain, but I will persist in trusting God, who has promised that even birds will not fall to the ground apart from his will. I long for the skill to build near the place of sacrifice, where the altar fire will shine through.

FATHER, THANK YOU FOR MY COMFORTABLE HOME WHERE
I CAN SLOW DOWN AND COMMUNE WITH FAMILY AND FRIENDS.
THANK YOU FOR ALWAYS KEEPING ME IN YOUR LINE OF VISION.
IN THE NAME OF "THE TRUE LIGHT, WHO GIVES
LIGHT TO EVERY MAN."
AMEN.

HAPPY FATHER'S DAY EVERYDAY

He tends his flock like a shepherd: He gathers the lambs in his arms and
carries them close to his heart; he gently leads those who have young.

ISAIAH 40:11

Sunday mornings in my childhood home were routine. My parents'
agenda included assembling with the saints and taking their little saints
with them. At some point in the morning ritual, my dad always reached
into his pocket and gave dimes to my sister and me. I liked getting my dime
early on Sunday morning so I could keep a small portion of the Lord's
money in my purse before giving it away with a cheerful heart. Fear was the
thing wrong with the idyllic scene.

If Dad waited too long to give us the dimes, one of us would remind
him, but it usually wasn't me. Although I was the older, my six-year-old
sister asked for the coins. My gentle dad sensed my timidity and once
asked me why. I shrugged my shoulders. The eight-year-old Cathy didn't
have an answer.

Later, in my pre-teen years, there were numerous assurances of Dad's
love for me, but none were more poignant than a life-threatening
situation: During a trip to Arkansas, we children became nauseated, and
Dad stopped at a pharmacy en route. After a conference call, a local doctor
prescribed sedatives to help us "sleep it off." No one suspected the cause
of our illness: carbon monoxide poisoning. A timely arrival in Arkansas
and the fresh mountain air quickly recuperated us.

During the return trip to Texas the symptoms recurred. My praying dad grew suspicious of the cars exhaust system. As we neared Nacogdoches, the situation became grave. My four-year-old brother was unconscious. Sherry and I, ten and twelve, were disoriented and scared.

Dad stopped and phoned the nearest hospital to alert them that he was bringing in his family. Upon our arrival, the emergency staff rushed out with two wheelchairs, and my siblings were whisked inside.

As I clumsily exited the car, my knees buckled, but Daddy's strong arms intervened. He scooped me up and snugged me to his chest. I remember thinking before I lost consciousness, "You'll be okay. Daddy has you." I recall a vivid dissipation of fear because of my father's encircling arms.

The heavenly Father is on a fear-removal mission. He is doing everything in his power to relieve Christians' and unbelievers' fears. Luke says he is even kind "to the ungrateful and wicked" (6:35). The ever-watchful Father often intervenes, rescues, soothes and saves. Worry lines need not collect on my brow.

God's arms encircle millions, but somehow his lap holds only one child at a time.

GOD OF MY CHILDHOOD, GOD UNTIL-THE-END, WHEN MY DAYS
ON EARTH ARE FINISHED, I LONG TO MOVE INTO YOUR HOUSE.
WITHOUT FEAR, I COME IN THE NAME OF JESUS,
WHO IS GETTING MY ROOM READY.
AMEN.

WHEN GOD SINGS

By day the LORD directs his love, at night his song is with me—
a prayer to the God of my life.

PSALM 42:8

As a young child, my daughter Sheryle loved to play with dolls. One morning in our kitchen, she came through the door wagging most of her babies. Pretending to be a mommy, she handed me a sick child and said, "Her fever is one hundred eight!" Sheryle frowned in concern.

Soon I became the doctor, and the kitchen turned into an infirmary. The other dolls caught the disease and were hospitalized. Chairs, placed seat-to-seat, became stretchers. When we ran out of beds, Sheryle suggested the oven in our freestanding range substitute as a hospital room. She placed two dolls on the wire shelf, kissed them, and closed the door. Most of the children recovered in half an hour. Soon distracted, play was abandoned, and we left the kitchen. The babies in the oven were forgotten.

Human forgetfulness is a common dilemma. Because of forgetting, I've burned food, paid late charges at the bank, neglected birthdays, lost untold items, and baptized the bathroom floor with sink-water several times. As age advances, the problem gets worse. God isn't forgetful like me.

Some folks accuse God of forgetting his creation. Psalmist David said the Creator could always see him, from the farthest galaxy to beneath the ocean floor (137:7-10). He also marveled about God being "mindful of him" (8:4). God always sees me too.

Back in my kitchen on another day, and ready to bake a batch of cookies, I turned the oven to the preheat setting. A plastic odor filled the room and smoke drifted upward. Popping the range door open, I discovered two scorched dolls. Like good parents, Sheryle and I soothed their wounds, cooed and sang over them as they "healed."

Adults need healing, too. Often trouble will twist me like a dishcloth and wring every ounce of energy down the drain. Zephaniah wrote "get-well" words to a suffering and worn-out Jerusalem and said: "Do not fear, O Zion; do not let your hands hang limp. The LORD... he will quiet you with his love, he will rejoice over you with singing" (3:16-17).

What a snapshot of God! Anytime I am tempted to think God has forgotten how hot it is down here, I need only remember these words of Zephaniah. The Consoler and Quieter is tuning up. Even today, he may be finding the perfect key to bring harmony to my life.

God may be getting ready to sing.

FATHER, THANK YOU FOR REMEMBERING AND SINGING OVER ME.
MAY HEAVEN'S CHORUS RING IN MY HEART. IN THE NAME OF
JESUS, WHO SANG HYMNS WITH HIS DISCIPLES.
AMEN.

FORECAST

He who speaks on his own does so to gain honor for himself, but he who works for the honor of the one who sent him is a man of truth: there is nothing false about him.

JOHN 7:18 THE WORDS OF JESUS

Abimelech and Isaac were two leaders of tribal families meeting to settle squabbles over wells of life-supporting water, a precious commodity. When Abimelech approached Isaac about making a peace treaty between them, one of his comments was, "We saw clearly that the Lord was with you" (Genesis 26:28).

Abimelech and his advisors saw how God blessed Isaac with a large inheritance, a wife, twin sons, many servants, livestock, and great wealth. Abimelech's words remind me of a longtime friend and mentor many lovingly called "Nannie." As newlyweds, my husband and I first met this silver-haired widow while we were looking for a church home. She quickly became my friend who, with her pattern of good works, taught me many things. Two particular life-lessons came from her example.

When she spoke to the women's class about the death of her husband, many of us younger women saw clearly that the Lord was with her. "Nannie" and her husband were on vacation in Hawaii when he died in his sleep. Before summoning for help, she knelt by their bed and gave thanks to God for their marriage. Far from home and relatives, prayer came before she reached out to others for comfort.

A second strong impression of her devotedness to God was a phrase she used in praying at a women's luncheon meeting. In her prayer, "Nannie" included a profession of faith. I remember her words, "And, Lord, I confess to you that I believe Jesus is the Christ, the Son of God." Her refreshing verbal affirmation of Christ as Lord serves even today as a reminder to revere Christ with words and actions.

Abimelech's words "[w]e saw clearly…" also made me think about weather forecasting. When my children were at home and Mama wasn't happy, they sometimes forecasted a warning, an "emergency broadcast" to seek shelter before the storm. Blustery outbursts and stormy households can change, and should. Christ-followers need to change to clear and sunny, where observers can clearly see lives yielding to the Holy Spirit.

As I grow older, I often wonder what my family and others observe in my life. Do they see me honoring the Lord? Do my friends expect to hear stories of God's intervention in my life, or do they hear whining about what went awry in my schedule?

I am still on the playing field. People are watching my actions, and I'm wondering what the view is from the bleachers.

LORD JESUS, YOU KNOW THAT HONORING THE FATHER MINUTE
BY MINUTE IS FULL TIME WORK, AND YOU ESTEEMED GOD
PERFECTLY. AID ME IN DOING THE SAME BECAUSE MANY
"SAW CLEARLY THE LORD WAS WITH YOU."
AMEN.

MAKING ROOM FOR ESSENTIALS

Watch out! Be on your guard against all kinds of greed; a man's life does not consist in the abundance of his possessions.

LUKE 12:15 THE WORDS OF JESUS

One dark, December evening, my family was readying to leave on a short holiday trip. We loaded our pickup with gifts, food and two children, Russell and Sheryle. The pickup had one bench seat. With two kids squeezed between us, my husband began driving toward Dallas.

Into the trip only a minute, Sheryle asked, "What's this furry thing sitting on my lap?" I immediately reached over and found the "furry thing" to be a very quiet farm kitten. We U-turned and dropped the feline off so she could spend Christmas with her siblings. We suspect the cat had been smuggled on board. For several reasons, it was expedient to get rid of non-essentials.

Our minister's sermon series "Living Rich Simply" prompted my husband and me to start eliminating household knick-knacks. Our shelves and cupboards overloaded, we decided non-essentials had to go because we are packing light for the rest of our earthly trip.

After a season of gift giving, we always have more possessions in our possession. For the future, one of my gift-giving goals is to buy gifts that take up temporary residence: soaps, fragrances, scented candles, money, food. Any item will be considered eligible for purchase if it can be consumed, melted down, sprayed out, burned up or spent in a year. I am strongly yearning for less in my house, and I suspect older friends and family are, too.

The accumulation in my home is not due entirely to gifts received. The other 364 days in a year contribute collections of cardboard rolls; twist-ties; the plastic thingumajig that broke off the whatchamacallit; junk mail; and all the extra buttons, knobs and nails saved for an emergency. Haven't needed them yet, but we are prepared.

David and I decided we're not collecting anything more than wrinkles this side of eternity. It's good that God will not allow the Messecars to take things out of this world. Heaven would look like Sanford's junkyard.

On earth I could get by with a lot less in order to do a lot more for Him. If I don't control possessions, they control me. I find myself dusting teapots instead of cooking stew for an ill neighbor, polishing silver instead of praying in my prayer garden. I need to watch for unnoticed hitchhikers.

When my adult daughter Sheryle visits home and says, "Mom, after you're gone, may I have the Prussian Princess figurine?" I say, "Why wait? She hasn't traveled in awhile. Take her now."

If all goes as planned, there will be fewer trinkets in the Messecar household. We've got to make room for all those wrinkles.

LORD GOD, SNUFF OUT MY DESIRE FOR POSSESSIONS. INCREASE MY DESIRE TO SEEK THE KINGDOM. IN THE NAME OF JESUS, WHO NEAR THE END OF HIS LIFE OWNED A ONE-PIECE TUNIC AND BEYOND THAT CLOTHING NOT MUCH ELSE.
AMEN.

CHAPTER 4

IN THE NAME OF JESUS NOTICING DUSTY FEET

THE ROYAL LAW

If you really keep the royal law found in scripture, "Love your neighbor as yourself," you are doing right.

JAMES 2:8

When my daughter Sheryle was ten, we stopped at a fast food restaurant in Houston for lunch. The dining room was filled almost to capacity, but we found two seats next to the rest rooms. Near the end of our meal, a teenage male employee began rolling a janitorial bucket and mop toward the rest rooms. The worker, dressed in his uniform of gray trousers and gray and white striped shirt, steered the sloshy contents with the mop handle. Approaching the rear of the restaurant where we sat, the young man began having a seizure. He fell to the floor and knocked over the bucket of water.

What could I do to help? The last time I witnessed someone having a seizure, several friends aided her with a substitute tongue depressor, to keep her from biting her tongue. I recalled that that medical aid was now outdated.

Everyone close by stopped eating. The boy continued to have what I guessed to be a grand mal seizure. Within seconds, another teenage employee yelled to the front, "John's having another seizure!"

At the first cry of alarm, a man stepped away from the crowded lunch counter and hurried toward the back. Dressed immaculately in a white shirt, gray flannel slacks, tie and textured jacket, he looked out of place in the casual, jeans-clad crowd. He calmly asked the other employee, "What's his name?"

"John," the employee answered.

On the floor, John's muscles were racked by spasms, his teeth chattered and his limbs jerked. The helper moved the mop bucket away from John's thrashing head to spare him further injury. Then squatting, he placed one knee in the water, bent over John and said, "I'm a doctor, John. You'll be okay."

Over and over he called John's name. He gently coached and assured him, "John, relax. This will be over soon. John, you're okay. Relax, John. This won't last much longer."

Again and again he encouraged the writhing boy. Finally, John's body, responding to internal signals and the soothing voice of the doctor, relaxed.

The close quarters and activity had confined the other diners and us to our seats. Sheryle and I gathered our remaining food and tiptoed through the puddled water to leave. The last thing John needed was a gawking crowd.

The picture of John and the physician remain vivid in my memory. One was in need of help, one was willing to step into the middle of things—*in medias res*—and extend compassion. My daughter and I witnessed the royal law that day when two pairs of gray trousers were soaked—one by circumstance, one by choice.

GOD OF KINDNESS, MAY I NEVER OUTLIVE MY LOVE FOR THE KING. MAY I FOLLOW HIS ROYAL EDICT TO LOVE MY NEIGHBOR. I ASK IN YOUR THRONE ROOM BECAUSE JESUS LEFT THE DOOR OPEN.

AMEN.

IMITATORS

I have loved you with an everlasting love;
I have drawn you with loving-kindness.

JEREMIAH 31:3

Pulling on work gloves, grabbing the cordless business phone, and walking out the back door, I readied to chase skittering leaves and tidy up our yard. The phone rang several times during the first hour I worked, and then it rang once more. I dropped the rake and ran to answer the phone; however, I stopped midway when I realized the ring emanated from an overhead branch of a pin oak. The ringing sound was an imitation. Remarkably close in sound to the real tone of the phone, a mockingbird trilled the phones ring.

"If you hear a cell phone ring outdoors, you may be startled to discover that the 'phone' has feathers," was the report in *National Geographic*, May 2002. A brief note about cellular phones explained that starlings were taught by the Romans to imitate human voices and today their repertoire includes other birdcalls, sirens, chain saws, horse whinnying, and now the warbling of cell phones.

With the outdoor use of mobile phones increasing, *National Geographic* predicts other mimics such as mockingbirds and mynahs will also be heard emulating ringing sounds. The next time I work in my yard, I will be carrying my cell phone outdoors because my ring-tone is "Ode to Joy." I can't wait for the copycat mockingbird to learn that tune.

To the Ephesians, Paul commends imitation, to imitate what they observe God doing in the same way "children learn proper behavior from their parents." Also Paul emphasizes learning from God and Christ by keeping "company with" them and learning a "life of love." Paul concludes his remarks about imitating God's love by saying, "Love like that" (Ephesians 5:1-2, The Message).

When I keep company with God, I learn better ways of imitating him. Sometimes we visit through prayer; at other times we visit through my study of his word. During the times when I'm his attentive student, I keep a yellow pad and a number two pencil ready to journal. The more often I visit my Teacher's classroom, the more often I'm exposed to his exorbitant love.

When I truly get to know the Teacher, then my life will ring true.

LORD GOD, YOU AUTHORED THE BOOK OF LOVE AND CAST JESUS IN THE LIVE PERFORMANCE. I MARVEL AT HIS UNBLEMISHED LIFE. PLEASE, I WANT A MAKEOVER. MAKE ME LOOK LIKE JESUS.

AMEN.

BREAD OF HEAVEN

I am the bread of life.

JOHN 6:48 THE WORDS OF JESUS

Every ten days I feed my sourdough bread starter whether it wants to eat or not. That's the beginning process for making bread at our house. Forty-eight hours later my family has three fresh loaves of the yummy-smelling bread.

Bread, a diet staple for mankind, is a mixture of grain and water. The earliest forms of bread were baked on hot stones. Egypt is credited with the first leavened bread and brick ovens. Yesteryear's coarse bread was nothing like today's commercially baked, enriched, sliced white bread.

In the 1900s in the United States, 95 percent of bread was baked at home. By 1950, commercial bakeries turned out 95 percent. When a child of 12 receives 75 percent of his calories from enriched bread, that amount is nutritionally sufficient for growth.

The Bread of Life is essential for good spiritual health. Jesus prescribed "daily requirements" when he said, "Man does not live on bread alone, but on every word that comes from the mouth of God" (Matthew 4:4).

On one occasion, a crowd rushed after Jesus. Caught up in the moment of chasing after Jesus, only one in 5000 plus remembered to bring along food. As the day grew long, Jesus noticed their hunger, and a young boy donated his food to Jesus, who in turn prayed over the crusts.

In Jesus' hands, several loaves became thousands, and the usual processes of sowing seeds, sprouting, maturing, harvesting, grinding, mixing and baking were bypassed. After the meal, Jesus tried to leave the crowd, but many still trailed after him.

He knew their hearts. "You are looking for me, not because you saw miraculous signs but because you ate the loaves and had your fill" (John 6:26). Not any different from people today, those crowds liked the quick fix for hungry bellies.

In this same setting, Jesus connected table bread and the bread of heaven to say about himself, "He who comes to me will never go hungry, and he who believes in me will never be thirsty" (6:35).

In elementary school, my class took a field trip to Mrs. Baird's bakery. I still remember the line of fourth graders with our noses aloft, sniffing the yeasty scented air. Enticed, we became instant Baird fans. After the tour, each student received a slice of hot, buttered bread. Melted butter on warm bread lingers in my memory and is probably the best straight-out-of-the-oven bread I've ever sampled.

As good as that slice tasted, it will never compare to the true Staff of Life, the Bread of Heaven, Jesus Christ.

FATHER, JESUS, OFTEN THE QUEST TO FILL MY STOMACH IS STRONGER THAN MY DESIRE FOR YOU. PLEASE REVERSE MY APPETITES, FOR YOU SATISFY LIKE NO MORSEL OF FOOD.
AMEN.

GETTING TO KNOW ELIZABETH

God sets the lonely in families.

PSALM 68:6

My friend Elizabeth was nearly 100 when she died. This petite woman with pale blue eyes always had a warm smile for visitors. Her favorite parting phrase for any helper was, "Thanks a million times over." To a stranger she looked like any other aging American, but Elizabeth had a story.

Nearly two years old, Elizabeth boarded a train in the city of New York bound for Texas. She was one of an estimated 300,000 orphans adopted by families throughout the United States, Canada and Mexico. Before a scheduled orphan train arrived in a community, upstanding citizens screened prospective families who wished to provide homes.

The movement of placing children in homes lasted from 1863 to early 1900's, and their families stay in touch through The Orphan Train Society based in Fayetteville, Arkansas. In 1905 the train whistle blew near Stoneham, Texas, alerting citizens that the orphan train had arrived. The Niscavits adopted one-year-old Elizabeth and another young boy of no kinship. Of Irish descent, Elizabeth arrived with a cloth birth certificate pinned to her dress, along with a round cardboard disk with the number 62 on it.

For most of her life, Elizabeth lived, attended school, and went to church within a mile of the rail tracks that brought her to Texas. During the majority of adult life, she cared for ill family members: her mother, father, and much later her husband and son. Her daughter—Genevieve— is her lone survivor.

Elizabeth requested that a few favorite items be buried with her. Placed at her feet were her wedding gown, veil, and the two cardboard circles with the numbers she and her adopted brother wore from New York.

On an autumn day, Elizabeth was laid to rest in Stoneham, less than a mile from the rail tracks. The sun shone brilliant and wind stirred chimes hanging in tree branches. As the final graveside prayer swept upward, a freight train wound its way south. An engineer, unaware of the part he played in the final tribute, blew the train horn. The sound was an appropriate farewell to the last-known orphan train survivor adopted by Stoneham families.

When Elizabeth was well and we visited, clock hands ran backwards, as I listened to her tell about Frank, who came courting on horseback, and about her wedding preparations and cooking for large family gatherings.

Getting to know Elizabeth was a distinct pleasure. She taught me many things about being devoted to family. If I could only bend close to her ear once more, I'd say, "Thanks a million times over."

FATHER, THANK YOU FOR CARING FOR THE FATHERLESS AND FOR ALLOWING ME TO ADOPT ELIZABETH AS MY FRIEND FOR THE LAST QUARTER OF HER LIFE. IN THE NAME OF JESUS, WHO COMMISSIONED JOHN TO TAKE CARE OF MARY AS IF SHE WERE HIS OWN MOTHER.
AMEN.

CHAPTER 5

IN THE NAME OF JESUS SAYING
"HOLD TO MY TEACHING"

THREE SECOND-CHANCES

Then the word of the Lord came to Jonah a second time: "Go to the great city of Nineveh and proclaim to it the message I give you." Jonah obeyed the word of the LORD and went to Nineveh.

JONAH 3:1-3A

Second chances. I'm thankful for them because there are very few occasions I get everything right the first time.

A red metal loom represents a second chance for which I'm grateful. When my younger sister and I were in elementary school, we used a red metal loom to stretch multi-colored loops of cotton over prongs to make potholders. Our first efforts were amateurish, missing more than a few of those loop-de-loops.

Later we became adept at creating a variety of designs, and we began selling them door-to-door, even though both of us were shy about meeting new people. After we knocked on the doors and before the homeowner answered, I usually ran behind nearby shrubbery, abandoning my poor sister to pitch the potholders to the woman-of-the-house, who probably had a drawer full of the same kind. I'm thankful my dear sister forgave me and remained my best friend despite my many desertions.

I'm also especially thankful for those who forgive me again and again when my side of the conversation lacks grace. Numbering the sins of my tongue would be like counting the hairs on a camel.

During the Vietnam War, my fiancé David brought news of the government's latest draft pick. Him. My heart had dreaded this moment.

Confronted with the reality that his number had come up, an inane cliché popped out of my mouth. "That's the way the cookie crumbles." I'm thankful the 20-year-old fellow looked into my eyes, saw love and chose to ignore my careless remark. He's given me numerous second chances for many years.

The grandest second chance of all is God's gift of slate-clean days. Every morning I wake up to new beginnings. Jeremiah reminds me that I awaken to fresh start dawns due to God's love. He wrote, "Because of the LORD's great love we are not consumed, for his compassions never fail. They are new every morning . . ." (Lamentations 3:22-23). Great is God's faithfulness.

I have made and will continue to make poor first impressions. A dowdy appearance, a sour attitude or stammering speech are blunders that may be hard to erase. They appear like bumps on the end of a nose, but I'm thankful for people who can get past my warts.

Above all, I am grateful to my multiple-chance Father.

THANK YOU, GOD, FOR KINDRED SPIRITS WHO LEARNED TO USE YOUR EYEGLASSES. PLEASE ENHANCE MY OUTLOOK ON OTHERS. IN THE NAME OF JESUS, WHO DOES NOT MAKE JUDGMENTS ON WHAT CAN BE SEEN OR TOUCHED.
AMEN.

25,000 WORDS

When words are many, sin is not absent,
but he who holds his tongue is wise.

PROVERBS 10:19

On average, women speak 25,000 words a day. I don't believe it. Who counted? Who held the calculator? Did someone record conversations then tediously count the words? Was a similar experiment conducted for men?

Please, men, be kind. I can almost hear the males' jovial response to the word count. "Is that all?" My female friends' reactions are totally the opposite. They think the number is astonishingly high. Me too.

Commandments about speech control abound in the proverbs. Some of Solomon's instructions are directed to women. He compares a quarrelsome wife to "a constant dripping on a rainy day" (27:15). Some of his wisdom words refer to men. "Do you see a man who speaks in haste? There is more hope for a fool than for him" (29:20).

The number of words certainly increases the frequency for sin, and fewer words are often the appropriate communication. Job told the Lord, "I put my hand over my mouth" (40:4). In a volley of irrational words, a hand moving toward an overflowing mouth is truly poetry in motion because spoken words launch a mission of instruction, blessing or destruction, and they will affect someone.

Hmmm. If I speak 25,000 words a day and there are 365 days in a year, multiplied by my age, the sum tallies up to slightly over 5 billion. Give or take a few nouns. Gulp.

Another challenge is pleasant conversations in my home. A sharp tongue should not be my legacy. Long ago, a relieved husband marked his wife's resting place, "Beneath this stone, a lump of clay, lies Arabella Young: who on the 21st of May began to hold her tongue."

Recently, I needed to apologize to my husband for the manner in which I answered him. After my apology, my husband said in his best martyr tone, "It's okay. I'm used to it."

One night after that, my bravado was running high and I asked David to rate my speech from one to ten, with one being "mostly mute" to ten being "a marathon talker." Recognizing trouble at both ends of the scale, my husband gave the perfect number.

If his answer had varied a digit or two, I had my hand ready—no, not to clamp over his mouth. I had it ready to dial our attorney, to tell him what to write on my tombstone.

LORD GOD, I DO BUILD A TOWER OF BABBLE SOMETIMES.
PLEASE FORGIVE ME AND SET A GUARD OVER MY MOUTH—
CHERUBIM WITH FLAMING SWORD IF NEEDED. TEACH ME
SILENCE OF THE TONGUE. I REMEMBER JESUS BEFORE PILATE
AS I ASK THESE BLESSINGS.
AMEN.

ON GROWING OLD

Do not cast me away when I am old;
do not forsake me when my strength is gone.

PSALM 71:9

The image of a lovely, gray-haired woman with her arms outstretched was captured in a photograph while she accepted a crowd's applause. This youthful looking woman stood near a table at a Christian fundraiser dinner. Her age revealed in a caption on the picture shocked me. She was 96 years old. According to the accompanying article, her sparkling countenance was unmistakably the result of a life given over to God.

The sprightly woman is my heroine. I can still close my eyes and see her face. Because she epitomizes my goal, I placed her picture on my refrigerator for almost a year. "Feeble and frail" may be in my future, but reflecting contentment from God despite life's circumstances is something I continually long for.

A psalm captures a metaphorical picture of seniors who depend on God:

> The righteous will flourish like a palm tree, they will grow
> like a cedar of Lebanon; planted in the house of the LORD,
> they will flourish in the courts of our God. They will still
> bear fruit in old age, they will stay fresh and green,
> proclaiming, 'The LORD is upright; he is my Rock, and
> there is no wickedness in him.' (Psalm 92:12-15)

Stereotypes of older people include brittle bones and loose, baggy skin. God's view of righteous old age is bearing fruit and staying "fresh and green." Moses is an example of an elderly "lush" leader. Abraham's cultivation produced an unwavering faith in God's plan, and even after these patriarchs passed the century mark, God arranged great tests and assignments for them.

I am reminded of a story from *Chicken Soup for the Woman's Soul*. A woman saw a poorly dressed child window-shopping. She escorted the child into the store and outfitted him with new clothes. Back on the sidewalk, the little boy asked, "Are you God, Ma'am?"

She smiled down at him, "No, son, I'm just one of his children."

Then the child reasoned, "I knew you had to be some relation."

Kinship with God is the key for senior citizen success. If I am physically healthy, I hope to keep serving others. If my physical health fails, I hope to revitalize others through phone calls, letters or e-mail. If my eyesight dims, I will listen for opportunities to lift others up with refreshing words. If I lose physical health, eyesight and hearing, I will finally dust off my rocking chair, but I plan to rock and pray, rock and pray!

ANCIENT LORD, MAY I FIND WAYS TO HONOR YOU
EVEN WHEN DUSK IS FALLING. THROUGH JESUS,
WHO IS LIFE AND RESURRECTION.
AMEN.

GROCERY STORE GREETINGS

From the east I summon a bird of prey; from a far-off land,
a man to fulfill my purpose.

ISAIAH 46:11

Too many things broke. Too many joints ached and too few dollars were earned that week. One day that week, I shopped in the grocery store and struggled with an agitating, tug-of-war grocery cart. My hurriedly scribbled grocery list looked like hieroglyphics to me.

Common cans of corn and beans were grabbed off shelves. The carts wheels continued to whine like a tired child as I coaxed the buggy toward the last aisles.

Rounding the corner of the frozen food section, an arctic blast nearly bowled me over. Shivering, I bent over and peered into the low, cool bins and tried to make a decision between Brussels sprouts or mustard greens. Worn out, lethargic and ice cold, I tried to function. God knew my state of mind and had a surprise waiting for me down by the pancakes.

Glancing up to warm my face, I saw a Christian woman named Dot. She saw me. Her eyes lit up, and a smile that would melt an ice cap spread across her face. She walked toward me, folded me up in her arms, squeezed me, and said with enthusiasm, "Cathy, God love her!"

My sagging spirit sprouted wings. We chatted, and in a few moments her husband Leffel joined us, and slipped his arm around Dot. My misery stayed somewhere between the frozen yogurt and the Popsicles.

Peter received a similar lift after his despairing days following Jesus' crucifixion. This disciple's dearest friend on earth had died, and Peter deserted him in his final hours. Regrets and what-ifs must have taunted Peter's every thought.

Sunday morning, victorious words were about to be sent Peter's way. Women visited the tomb of Jesus and heard an angel say: "He is risen! . . . . But go, tell his disciples and Peter." The on-purpose Lord sent a personal message to his sorrowing friend. The message must have relieved Peter's sad heart.

God encourages his children even when the umpire Satan is crying "You're out!" The heavenly Father is the ultimate designer of revitalization—through the words of a hymn, a mockingbird's song, a new insight about Jesus, an embrace, a raindrop, or perhaps a psalm. A total list of all the ways he encourages is impossible to pen. Every day, God pulls on my heartstrings and the motion is upward.

My Father knows when I need a break from Satan's discouraging tactics. That's when he steps into my world and tilts my chin up so my eyes are focused on him. Sometimes, he even plants his messengers—schooled in love—in the aisle of a grocery store.

THANK YOU, LORD GOD, FOR THE STARS YOU FLUNG TO EARTH,
THE PEOPLE WHO BRING SPARKLE TO MY UNIVERSE.
IN THE NAME OF JESUS, WHO INVITED THE BONE-TIRED AND
SOUL-INFLICTED TO COME TO HIM.
AMEN.

CHAPTER 6

IN THE NAME OF JESUS THE BRIDEGROOM

LOVE SHINE

So Jacob served seven years to get Rachel, but they seemed
like only a few days to him because of his love for her.

GENESIS 29:20

When I least expect, the textbook on life opens and an acquaintance does something that knocks the wind out of one of my bad habits. I recently had the pleasure of learning a better way of communicating with my husband because of such an occurrence.

Through our business, we met a couple who speaks more kindly to each other than any other married couple we have met. Their names are Buck and Jan Graham. When they interact and address each other by pet names, the tone of their speech is filled with admiration. My husband and I love to hear either of them call the other "Precious."

Recently in our home my husband asked me, "What's that noise?" The ringer on our business phone was turned off, and I heard the answering machine recording a message. He'd heard the sound many times before, but our hearing isn't what it used to be. The volume is up on everything, and yet we are hearing less.

My reply, "It's the answering machine," was less than cordial. Immediately, I regretted the tone of "you-should-know-what-that-sound-is."

I thought about married couples falling into language ruts, especially of replying with a grumble or flippant answer to mates. Climbing out of the bad-habit trench and getting back on the grassy terrain of pleasant words and nuances can often be difficult.

Later I apologized to David and said, "I'd like to be more like the Grahams. They're always so nice to each other." My intentions were good, but before long I once again gave David an answer with an attitude. He looked at me with a smile and said, "Thank you, Precious." Laughter rippled up my throat and erupted in a full blown smile.

Since that moment, when either of our words to each other is curt, one of us will address the other during our conversation with the name "Precious." It's a gentle reminder of the love pact we made long ago to honor each other.

Jesus encouraged his followers to allow his love to shine through the windows of their everyday lives: "You are the light of the world... let your light shine before men, that they may see your good deeds and praise your Father in heaven" (Matthew 5:14-16).

Thank you Buck and Jan, for letting the brilliance of your love shine.

FATHER, THANK YOU FOR DESIGNING MARRIAGE. WILL YOU GARDEN IN MY HEART TODAY? LOOSEN MY ROOT-BOUND SELF-CENTEREDNESS. PLEASE MIST THE PARCHED PATCHES OF INDIFFERENCE. FOR MY FRIENDS, BRING LASTING GROWTH TO NEWLYWEDS AND TO LONGTIME MARRIED LOVERS. IN THE NAME OF THE BRIDEGROOM. AMEN.

A TOAST TO ROBUST MARRIAGES

Isaac brought her into the tent of his mother Sarah, and he married Rebekah. So she became his wife, and he loved her; and Isaac was comforted after his mother's death.

GENESIS 24:67

"Going to the chapel and we're gonna get married . . . going to the chapel of love." The lyricist added words about ringing bells, sun shining and everlasting love.

If only married life were always as perfect as sentimental love songs. One of the men in my home congregation quotes W. C. Fields and says with a twinkle in his eye, "There are three kinds of rings in a marriage: the engagement ring, the wedding ring and the suffering."

When David and I planned to marry, we went to talk with my parents. Jittery about the parental conference, we walked into my family's den with me cowering behind David's tall frame.

We honestly thought our news would surprise my parents, but they had noticed our growing affection. Mother was ironing, and Daddy was talking to her. When they saw our serious countenances, they gave us their full attention and later their permission to marry. Within fourteen months, my preacher-dad presided at our wedding ceremony.

I don't recall many of the words Daddy said on our wedding day because tulle, lilies, trousseau, and groom were on my mind, but I do recall with clarity what Dad told us the night we asked permission to get married.

With loving concern he said, "When two Christians marry, later if there is serious trouble between them, one or both of them have stopped being Christ-like." For our marriage, Dad's wise words and Jesus' example have been our ideal.

Jesus was able to love with all his heart because of his communion with God and the Holy Spirit. He then took strength from their relationship and sincerely served others. If only everyone could be wed to God before taking marriage vows.

At the wedding feast in Cana, Jesus' mother noticed that the host was about to be embarrassed by a shortage of wine. She alerted Jesus to the situation and then told the house servants, "Do whatever he tells you." His presence at that wedding turned plain water into a wine rich miracle.

If I always followed Mary's directive to the servants—listening to Jesus and doing whatever he tells me—my marriage would be even better. We invited Jesus to be Master of Ceremonies on our wedding day, and now he's with us through hospitalizations and good cholesterol reports, overdrawn notices and abundant bank accounts, in sickness and in health, for richer, for poorer, until death do us part.

FATHER, I COME IN THE NAME OF THE SINGLE, DEVOTED LORD.
EVEN AFTER MANY YEARS OF MARRIAGE, I FIND MYSELF AT TIMES
WATERING DOWN YOUR COMMANDS. PLACE ON MY HEART THE
DESIRE TO DO WHATEVER JESUS TELLS ME.
AMEN.

THE TREASURES

Do not store up for yourselves treasures on earth . . . But store up
for yourselves treasures in heaven . . . For where your treasure is,
there your heart will be also.

MATTHEW 6:19-21

In the late 1960s, Mom and I were traveling north on I-45 in our pickup loaded with household items when the "special" box flipped out. The large container landed across the middle stripe on our side of the four-lane interstate. We were in the midst of a move because Dad and Mom's new house was ready. My husband was in Vietnam and I still lived with my parents.

When the box flew out, Mom pulled over. Before she cautioned me, I bailed onto the pavement, scanned the traffic, and darted to the middle of the road. Scooping up the box and scooting off the freeway, I hugged the container until I tied it securely in the back of the truck. My beaded white dress, worn two months earlier at my wedding, was in the hermetically sealed box.

The dress was a treasure then, but after several decades it's not as valued. Risking my life on a freeway to rescue the white gown is no longer viable. As a new bride, my treasures were still satin and lace. As a seasoned wife, my treasure is my husband's laughter. As a grandmother, my treasures have peanut-butter-smudged faces, and I have FBI-quality-finger-printed windows.

What did Jesus treasure? Jesus revered the Father, even missing sleep to spend time with him. Jesus cherished adults. Their distresses caused him pain and brought him to tears. He loved children, understanding their innocence and vulnerability. He also treasured truth and integrity and blessed all his companions through his presence.

In the gospel accounts, Jesus and his relationships seem to be a common theme, while his connections to the belongings of this world are minimized. From the rented feed trough to the gifted tomb, he owned little in between. Detached from possessions, he had time for a holy fixation on God and people.

When we moved into our current house, the kitchen had 39 cabinet doors and 11 drawers. I fell in love with shelf paper. A wiser woman cautioned me about too much space, "You'll just fill them up."

"No," I thought. "Never." The wise woman's prophecy came true. Now, too many heirloom linens, teacups and luncheon plates rest in nooks and crannies.

The more possessions I own, the more time I spend shuffling clutter and dusting inanimate objects. Possessions are jealous thieves demanding attention, leaving me less time to invest in people.

How do "good deeds" and "putting others first" travel beyond the stars and settle in the vaults of heaven? I don't know the answer, but I know God is packing the heavenly cupboards with what I'm sending ahead, not what I'm dusting below.

LORD GOD, PRY MY FINGERS FROM TANGIBLES. PLEASE GIVE ME THE SAVIOR'S 20/20 VISION. HELP ME NEVER TO SHELVE MY HUSBAND, CHILDREN, GRANDCHILDREN, FAMILY, OR FRIENDS IN FAVOR OF BAUBLES. IN THE NAME OF THE PILLOWLESS JESUS. AMEN.

A MEAL WITH LOVE

Better a meal of vegetables where there is love
than a fattened calf with hatred.

PROVERBS 15:17

When my husband and I were newlyweds, we paid our first rent in Junction City, Kansas, near Fort Riley. The apartment was in an old house, divided into seven units. Seven oversized closets. Standing still, David could touch the kitchen walls in every direction. In the hall near the bathroom, the refrigerator hummed its frosty tune. Not the perfect floor plan. Because we'd spent little married time together, our first home seemed a palace to us.

David had mailed me many letters from Louisiana, Georgia and Vietnam during the first 18 months of our long distance marriage. We were together less than 60 days after we said, "I do." After too few wedded-bliss days, but plenty of wedded-miss months, we were delighted with our apartment. Turning a corner in our cubbyhole and bumping into each other was pleasant, but wedding cake doesn't last forever, and we had a few newlywed misunderstandings.

The greatest miscommunication came after five months of shared quarters. Scheduled for only a half day of guard duty at the army base, David said as he left the apartment, "I thought we'd eat out for lunch."

I responded positively to his suggestion. By mid-morning, I put on a clean outfit, teased my hair into an appropriate height for the late 1960s, and awaited his arrival. About noon he came home, and I noticed a quick look of puzzlement cross his face that he didn't explain. As he changed out of his fatigues, we chatted cheerfully. Then he timidly asked, "Where's lunch?"

You could have knocked me over with a stalk of celery. I was stunned. Finally I managed to ask, "I thought you said we were going out to eat?"

He replied sheepishly, "I meant we'd go out of doors to eat. I thought we'd go on a picnic." I changed plans and clothes, threw together sandwiches and squashed my uptown-hair down to country-picnic-plain.

As we drove, David explained that we needed to see the Kansas landscape while we could. "We'll just cruise around until we find a shady picnic spot."

The Kansas landscape looked pretty much the same. Treeless. Finally pulling off the road, Dave opened the tailgate on our 1965 Chevy truck. We watched Kansans drive by as we washed down sticky peanut butter sandwiches with soda pop. Sitting on the tailgate with our legs swinging, we ate in the great outdoors.

Whether Dave and I dine at a mahogany dining table or off a tailgate, love must be in our table setting because in marriage some days are picnics and some days are Blue Plate Specials.

LORD GOD, EVERY DAY, YOU PREPARE A TABLE BEFORE DAVID AND ME. MAY WE ALWAYS RECOGNIZE YOU AS BOTH HOST AND GUEST. IN THE NAME OF JESUS, WHO BROUGHT YOUR BOUNTY INTO IMPROMPTU PICNICS.

AMEN.

TRUE LOVE

Be imitators of God, therefore, as dearly loved children
and live a life of love....

EPHESIANS 5:1-2

Pearl S. Buck, in her book *A Bridge For Passing,* writes about her husband's death. During her mourning, she received many condolences from around the world. Many notes of concern affirmed others' sorrow and love. She later returned to Japan to continue work on a film, *The Big Wave* that was in production when he died.

Upon her return to Japan, her friends offered comfort in a different manner from the expressions received in the states. She explains the distinction in this excerpt:

> In Tokyo nothing was said, yet everything was conveyed.
> Consideration was delicate but complete. My room in the hotel was
> bright with flowers and baskets of fruit. The little maids were ever
> present and solicitous. I understood, for in Japan even love is not
> to be expressed in words. There are no such words as "I love you"
> in the Japanese language. "How do you tell your husband that you
> love him?" I once asked a Japanese friend. She looked slightly
> shocked, "An emotion as deep as love between husband and wife
> cannot be put into words. It must be expressed in attitude and act."
> Nor or there equivalents of our love words—sweetheart, darling,
> dear, and all the rest.

Ms. Buck's example of how the Japanese conveyed love toward her reminds me of Jesus. As far as my memory serves, there is no record in the gospels of Jesus speaking the words "I love you." In John 15, Jesus did, however, give the command to "[l]ove each other" (vs. 17).

At some time in our culture, the philosophy arose that authentic love needs verbalization. Sincere words of love are endearing, but if they are not supported by minutes, hours, and days of "attitude and act," they become unmelodious, clanging cymbals.

Clanging cymbals, bells, more whistles—no thank you. Give me charity—real, live devotion.

FATHER, CURB MY HOLLOW WORDS LIKE, "LET ME KNOW IF I CAN DO ANYTHING." STOP ME MID-SENTENCE WHEN I BEGIN LIP SERVICE ONLY. MAY JESUS PERFORM HIS HANDS-ON LOVE THROUGH ME.

AMEN.

CHAPTER 7

IN THE NAME OF JESUS THE SABBATH WORKER

THE DODGE BLESSING

If you love those who love you, what reward will you get? ... And if you
greet only your brothers, what are you doing more than others?

MATTHEW 5:46-47

We kissed the Dodge goodbye and wept. Not literally, but when one
drives a vehicle for nearly a decade, memories cling to it like mud on
fenders. Two recollections stand out.

One is a collision in a small Texas town. An 88-year-old rammed my
Dodge with his green Ford LTD, but the Lord provided a safe haven for my
friend Doris and me, who were returning from a conference in Abilene.

At the crash site, I stood shakily by my severely damaged Dodge Ram
Charger while local citizens whispered to me that this same older
gentleman had wiped out the Pizza Hut drive-thru the week before. I
gathered from their whisperings that this head-on collision with my
vehicle was his third strike that month.

Stranded for eight hours in this small Texas town, we met many
interesting folk, including a female wrecker driver who took us to her
home. Ironically, she was married to the local grave digger. We were glad
to be alive and shaking his hand.

The other memorable event in which my Dodge had a part occurred
late one summer. I had asked God to allow me to help the poor in our
community in a physical way beyond monetary support. Within two
weeks I learned about a childless, older couple experiencing severe
problems. I visited them, and the husband's suffering was evident.

Disabled by untreated diabetes, his leg was gangrenous, and the odor from his infection filled their house. The couple had no medical insurance or money for an ambulance, but he needed to see a doctor immediately.

Despite his weakened condition, he consented to ride in the enclosed back area of my Dodge if only his wife and I could lift him inside. Finally, we accomplished this feat, and he settled into the larger space. We propped his legs with pillows, but he grew weaker by the moment in the sweltering September heat.

Arriving at the doctor's office, I went inside and asked if the doctor could make a curbside call. Our patient was far too weak to be moved again. The kind doctor, after tending to his patient in my Dodge, phoned the hospital and alerted them to prepare a gurney. When we arrived, nurses were compassionate and caring, but hospital insurance regulations forbade their lifting a patient from a private vehicle to a gurney. Once more God gave the 70-year-old wife and me the strength to lift her 200-pound husband.

He only lived a month after receiving medical care, but during that month the couple's small, extended family rallied to assist and comfort them.

I'm in awe of the way God chooses to honor my requests when I verbally and mentally assent to do his will. He never fails to locate a recipient. I am privileged to serve Jesus by taking good news to the poor and assisting him in binding up the broken hearted.

As a twenty-first century, mobile Christ follower, my calling is to use my vehicles—old Dodge or new one—to drive in his footsteps.

ABBA, ABBA, INFUSE ME WITH COMPASSION FOR THE LESS FORTUNATE. PLACE THEM IN MY PATH. IN THE NAME OF THE SABBATH WORKER. AMEN.

THE BALANCING ACT

*Even youths grow tired and weary...but those who hope
in the Lord will renew their strength.*

ISAIAH 40:30-31

Driving by the fairgrounds, I scan the advertisement. CIRCUS IN
TOWN, Main Attraction, Cathy. Why am I not surprised? Just balancing a
family's schedule any average day requires a super-duper juggling act.
Throw in a few "unexpecteds," such as a broken tooth, toilet or Toyota,
and I'm again the star of a three-ring-show.

Schedules are a big concern in many cultures. Recent magazine cover
blurbs lured shoppers, "Starved for Sleep?" One suggested "Unclutter Your
Home on a Weekend." Between the glossy covers, there may be several
hints to energize my body or streamline my life. But advice on how to pare
down my activities and fulfill my purpose on earth probably will not be
found in a popular magazine. To find that valuable information, I look to
The Creator and humbly whisper, "Help."

For three intense years, Jesus' itinerary was full of crowds, demands
and so-called "interruptions." In *Walk With Me*, Prentice Meador and Bob
Chisolm comment on the gospel of Mark and write about the incredible
pace of Jesus' life. They note that in Mark (RSV), the word "immediately"
appears frequently in reference to Jesus' next activity. In the other combined
gospels, the word is used only 11 times. In Mark, it is used 42 times.

In the book of Mark, consider a few of the times Jesus' plans went awry:
when he was looking for solitude (1:35-37); teaching a lesson (2:1-12);

trying to eat (3:20-21); seeking some rest (4:35-41); preparing to speak (5:21-34); and making plans with friends (6:30-34).

Jesus even had divine appointments while on the cross. His pain and agony were infringed upon, but he received strength to reach out to the thieves, save the responsive one, and make final living arrangements for his mother.

Was Jesus busier than I am? Most likely, but he handled each occurrence in his ministry as an opportunity and not an interruption.

LORD GOD, HELP ME WATCH FOR WAYS TO BE A SERVANT, FOR NOTHING IS MORE IMPORTANT THAN BEING ABOUT MY FATHER'S BUSINESS. IN THE NAME OF JESUS, WHO SAID TO HIS DISCIPLES, "PEACE BE WITH YOU!"
AMEN.

A WHOLE BUNCH OF NOTHING

But as for me and my household, we will serve the Lord.

JOSHUA 24:15

At a writing critique group, one of the members told a story. Late one night, while writing his latest Christian novel, he grew weary and began to get sleepy. He persisted in typing at his computer in order to capture a few final thoughts. He felt alert enough to continue but, nevertheless, he drifted off to sleep at the keyboard. After several minutes had lapsed, he awakened to find his finger had pressed the "o" key the entire time. Scrolling back through the manuscript, Don said, "I had forty pages of nothing."

Life may imitate Don's experience.

A PBS serial program, "Frontier House," filmed the activities of several modern families who agreed to live in Montana for a time. They were allowed the same conveniences available to settlers in the late 1800s. When these families returned to living in 2002, they were surprised to find they actually missed some of the 1800s living arrangements. Although they were happy to have modern conveniences again—running water, bathrooms, supermarkets, and cars, they missed the simplicity of their frontier lives.

Close quarters contributed to the tension in their simulated country living, but when they returned to their larger homes, the families found they missed the intimacy of the smaller dwellings. Also, they missed working together and the winter-survival chores like growing vegetables, canning, haymaking, storing of animal feed and chopping wood. Daily or seasonal activities performed for the good of the family nurtured unity, closeness and harmony.

The PBS "backwoods" adventures revealed that modern men may get trapped in their computerized lives and forget that loving relationships are most important.

Many stories in the Bible portray families loving God and each other. Joshua challenged his fellow tribesmen to "fear the LORD and serve him with all faithfulness" and to throw away the gods their ancestors had worshiped in Egypt. As a leader in Israel and his family, Joshua set the highest standard. "But as for me and my household, we will serve the LORD."

Many gods beckon for my family's time. I don't want my family to get worn out from chasing "idol" dreams, doze off and sleep through important years. If external pressures dictate the "when, where and how" of my family life, decades later we may find all we have is a whole bunch of nothing.

FATHER, WHEN MY FAMILY STRAYS FROM THE WAY, PLEASE TAP
MY SHOULDER. GET MY ATTENTION. LEAD MY HUSBAND,
CHILDREN AND GRANDCHILDREN IN PATHS OF RIGHTEOUSNESS
FOR YOUR NAMESAKE. I ASK THROUGH YOUR SON, WHO
EXCHANGED LIVING QUARTERS WITH YOU TO LIVE
ON EARTH WITH US.
AMEN.

PREMEDITATED LIFE

Morning by morning, O LORD, you hear my voice; morning by morning I lay my requests before you and wait in expectation.

PSALM 5:3

A friend phoned a local restaurant for carry-out hamburgers. She needed them in ten minutes, and she wanted to pick them up at exactly 5:18 p.m. This tortured, hamburger mom has one speed: overdrive. Every minute of her life is stressed and stretched. Like mine, her appointment book of life really comes unglued when the flu bug visits, termites invade or the agitated washer gives up the ghost.

The word "premeditated" is most often associated with "premeditated murder." However, when I overbook my day, I am murdering my peace of mind. Over-scheduling nearly always excludes time for spiritual nourishment and is a precursor for early gray hairs and grave.

An example of overbooking is my schedule. Far too often, I plan a vigorous day that would slay the most fit football jock. I draft and expect a blueprint day, and then I'm indignant if any tampering occurs.

One of my favorite children's songs expresses a great deal of wisdom in four sentences: "Good morning, God. This is your day. I am your child. Show me the way." This sweet melody expresses the need for Sovereign guidance and relinquishment of my part in the dawning day to eternal control.

When I think back over the past year of my life and search for the happiest day—one in which I experienced tranquillity, peace and goals accomplished—my mind zeroes in on one. I am not surprised to find the day was under-booked.

When my head is pillowed tonight, I plan to "premeditate" tomorrow. My day will include the have-to-do household things, personal business and a quiet time. For a change, I'll leave a few spaces blank, to make room for the Lord to work and time for the Lord to nudge me to invite a neighbor for coffee or jot a note to the homebound.

When my eyes pop open in the morning, the first thing I want to say is "Today is yours. Surprise me, Lord."

CREATOR OF TIME, PLEASE BE MERCIFUL AND HELP ME SAY
"NO" TO TIME THIEVES. GRANT ME WISDOM IN SPENDING THE
DAYS YOU HAVE PLACED IN MY ACCOUNT. IN THE NAME OF JESUS,
WHO ACCOMPLISHED IN 33 YEARS ALL THE WORK YOU
PLANNED FOR HIM.
AMEN.

CHAPTER 8

IN THE NAME OF JESUS LONGING FOR THE BLIND TO SEE

THE RED GIDEON BIBLE

One of them, when he saw he was healed, came back, praising God
in a loud voice. He threw himself at Jesus' feet and thanked him—
and he was a Samaritan.

LUKE 17:15-16

Stacks of Bibles lay neatly on a table when children entered their public elementary school cafeteria. The eyes and mouths of these little ones popped open when they saw the small red New Testaments the Gideons delivered.

After school, my seven-year-old daughter Sheryle was delighted when she raced in the door with her gift from the Gideons. Breathless, Sheryle told her story, "They had little red Bibles on the table, Mom! A woman told us they couldn't pass them out, but if we wanted to pick one up we could. No one wanted to go first, so I took a Bible, then all the other children followed." After hearing her account of the day, I lavished praise on her.

At age 14, Sheryle brought her Gideon Bible to me again and admitted she was not the first child to take a Bible. She had finagled my praise when she was seven. I don't know all the underlying reasons she lied, but I learned from her confession that she desired my applause.

I decided to make sure my family received genuine praise when they exhibited godly characteristics. After our talk, I laid the Bible in a prominent place for a visual reminder to praise my family.

Thinking about the matter after that incident, I considered the importance of expressing thanks and praise to family and friends. The ultimate way God fulfills his children's need for affirmation is through his direct expressions of love and sending the Savior Jesus. But he also sends pats-on-the-back from companions.

Paul wrote to his friend and fellow Christian Philemon and praised him for working with local believers, "Your love has given me great joy and encouragement, because you, brother, have refreshed the hearts of the saints" (vs. 7). In my community, home, and church I want to remember to say, Thank you, to God's workers.

The objects of my praise reveal my values. Here is the praise test I designed for myself. My human nature praises clothing, beauty, cars, homes, school grades, salaries, physical feats, social positions, jewelry and hairstyles. That list matches a list of the world's status symbols.

In contrast, this list reflects God's character: honesty, integrity, controlled tempers, helping the poor, justice, mercy, forgiveness or hospitality. My praises for others should reflect God's values, and any compliment I receive should spur me on to "love and good deeds."

Sheryle doesn't live with us anymore. She married and now has a home of her own. Before she left I returned the red Gideon Bible to her—with a gold ribbon tied around it. A note tucked inside encourages this dear, young woman to remember her praise manners as she and her husband establish their Christian home.

DEAR LORD, I OFTEN FORGET TO THANK YOU FOR BASICS—FOR AMBIDEXTROUS FINGERS, TOES FOR BALANCE, PROTECTIVE SKIN. YOU AMAZE ME WITH YOUR UNPRECEDENTED BOUNTY. MAY "THANK YOU" BE A CONSTANT COURTESY IN MY LIFE, TO YOU AND OTHERS. IN THE NAME OF JESUS. AMEN.

IS GOD PRAISING US?

How can you believe if you accept praise from one another, yet make no effort to obtain the praise that comes from the only God?

JOHN 5:44

A young mother told me about a conversation with her five-year-old son: "We were talking about praising God, and Jimmy said, 'I want God to praise me.' I told him God doesn't praise us; we praise Him."

As I listened to her, a scripture came to mind, John 5:44, where Jesus reminded the Jews to seek God's praise. I encouraged this young mother to assist her son in seeking God's praise. Later, I gave the subject extra thought and came up with a list of praise statements from God.

Jesus praised his forerunner: "I tell you the truth: Among those born of women there has not risen one greater than John the Baptist" (Mt. 11:11).

God testified concerning Israel's King: "I have found David son of Jesse a man after my own heart" (Acts 13:22).

God praised his servant Job: "There is no one on earth like him; he is blameless and upright, a man who fears God and shuns evil" (Job 1:8).

Jesus said of a repentant woman: "Her many sins have been forgiven—for she loved much" (Luke 7:47).

Jesus pointed out the strong belief of a Roman centurion: "I have not found anyone in Israel with such great faith" (Mt. 8:10).

These believers were praised for their devotion to God, but not flattered for inherited beauty, physical strength, outward adornment or job status. A psalmist explains what does and does not please God: "His pleasure is not in the strength of the horse, nor his delight in the legs of a man; the LORD delights in those who fear him, who put their hope in his unfailing love" (147:10-11).

When God looks down on my patch of earth, he doesn't care whether I'm wearing the latest fashion or an outdated coat, bell bottoms or Dockers, polyester or cashmere. My rank in the corporate world, cashier or CEO, is of little importance. God doesn't compare my physical strength to others or take notice if some are brawny and I am a wimp. Suntans and Mercedes will not impress him. I'm not on a fashion runway with God in the audience.

Sometimes, though, I picture God unlatching my heart and strolling through. Ouch! As I observe him reading my thoughts, I wish I had swept out the sorry attitudes. As he walks into a brighter corner of my sanctuary, I see him applauding the time I defended the oppressed. A blessing sounds from his lips when he sees I confessed his name before men.

Jimmy, thank you for the reminder to seek the praise of God.

JEHOVAH, YOU ALONE ARE TRULY WORTHY OF PRAISE, YET YOU
CHEER MY FEEBLE EFFORTS. THANK YOU FOR BEING A HEART-
WATCHER AND NOT A FASHION OBSERVER. IN THE NAME OF
RABBI JESUS, WHO WORE YOUR CLOAK OF PRAISE.
AMEN.

PRAISE HIM, PRAISE HIM

Let everything that has breath praise the LORD.

PSALM 150:6

Moses levied a complaint against the Hebrews: "You grumbled in your tents..." (Deuteronomy 1:27). He put them on notice about criticism toward God. As I read his warning to them, I wondered how many complaints arise from my climate-controlled home.

My multiple-blessed life is far too often accompanied by complaints. The Hebrews protested about their journey and God's provision, and nothing about human nature has changed in all these years. Like the Hebrews, at times, I still want what I don't have.

My home has many more comforts than a dusty nomad's tent, yet my complaints often revolve around my abundance. I gripe that clothing is the wrong color, is too tight or has scratchy tags. Advanced medical care is available and I fuss about long waits, hospital food and high bills. I argue that democracy in America is taken for granted. I bemoan too many political ads and what the free press reports. Any privilege can be named but, most likely, I can find something about it that doesn't quite fit my tastes.

My grousing needs to be replaced with praise. Praise means to bow low in the spirit to God, to acknowledge in my heart and my words God's sovereignty, to acknowledge he is worthy of praise for who he is, not only for the benefits he has given me.

Praise for God changes me. For example, when I praise him for who he is, I am steered back toward what really matters. When I focus on the holy goodness of God and how he designs individual blessings, griping grinds to a halt. When I recall the constant care from God, fussiness is finished. My hope in him is reborn.

David's example shows me that praise can change my perception of events. His praise psalm about God's rescue begins, "If the LORD had not been on our side" and concludes by saying, "Our help is in the name of the LORD, the Maker of heaven and earth" (124:1, 8). David didn't wallow in the mud of his misery. Through praise, he lifted his thoughts from the disaster at hand to the mighty hand of God.

Praise also prepares me for further obedience. When praise resonates in my heart, God tugs me toward his way of thinking. He takes my mind off me, me, me. He laces up my work shoes and gets me back on the servant track. When my praises rise to God, they become mental-joggers as God's attributes are recounted back to him. They affirm to me that he is both Lord and servant.

When the Lord looks down on my home and tunes in on my conversations and thoughts, may he hear praise! May I "sing to him, sing praise to him" and "tell of all his wonderful acts" (Psalm 105:2).

GIVER OF ALL GOOD THINGS, YOU ARE THE ROCK, LIVING WATER, REDEEMER, SERVANT AND FRIEND. PLEASE OPEN MY EYES, HOLY ONE, SHEPHERD, RESCUER AND HEALER. IN THE NAME OF JESUS, WHO LONGED FOR THE BLIND TO SEE. AMEN.

THE UNIVERSE AND MINOR DETAILS

How precious to me are your thoughts, O God! How vast is the sum of
them! Were I to count them, they would outnumber the grains of sand.

PSALM 139:17-18

Our family's two favorite "fly" stories cannot compare to the plague of flies
that swarmed into Egypt long ago. But let me tell you our stories anyway.

Needing lodging and food on a trip, my parents spent the night in a
town whose local economy was boosted by chicken farmers. They
searched for a restaurant and found a pizza parlor. After their eyes
acclimated to the dim interior, they were horrified to see many houseflies
in the restaurant. Thinking dining might be risky Mom said, "It's just too
dark in there to eat pizza."

They finally ordered a takeout supper from KFC. To combat the horde
of pests, the restaurant even had a bug zapper inside the dining area. My
folks could hear chicken and flies frying. An employee swept up dead flies
the entire time they waited for their order.

Another family "fly" story is David's and mine. Once a month we drive
to New Mexico to buy alfalfa. The county where we buy our hay has many
dairies, some with Holstein herds numbering over 1000, and the flies are
prolific during summer months.

Throughout a summer, we checked into our favorite motel with plenty of
big rig parking. Another guest always checked in on the same day. He hauls
cattle carcasses convertible-style, from a meat packing plant. His cargo
attracted thousands of flies, whole families, clans and cousins. We made

frantic efforts to get inside our room without the winged invaders. I will spare more details, except for one—we did not leave home without a fly swatter.

In no way do our family's experiences measure up to the Exodus 8, skin-crawling account of fly invasion. By God's mighty hand, judgment came upon Egypt. "Dense swarms of flies poured into Pharaoh's palace and into the houses of his officials, and throughout Egypt the land was ruined by the flies" (24). Bug zappers and fly swatters would have been useless.

As promised, God raised a barrier around the Hebrews—a "no-fly" zone. "But on that day I will deal differently with the land of Goshen, where my people live; no swarms of flies will be there...."

When Moses prayed for the pesky insects to leave Egypt, the Lord performed another miracle. "The flies left Pharaoh and his officials and his people; not a fly remained."

From this story in Israel's history, several facts emerge about God. He is able to engineer circumstances to gain glory for himself. His thoughts are in tune with his creation. His works are complete, such as ridding places of every single fly. His children often receive special protection, and he is not too busy to remember the small things in their lives.

The vast scope of God's workings is unfathomable. His creative nature striped zebras, spotted leopards, plumed parrots and redeemed man. He created galaxies and raindrops. Every day I receive personal care from Almighty God, God of the universe and minor details.

FATHER, THANK YOU FOR TUNING IN ON MY LIFE, FROM LOST KEYS TO LOST FRIENDS. YOU HEAR MY PLEAS AND MEET ALL MY NEEDS. THERE IS NONE LIKE YOU. THROUGH IMMANUEL, YOUR EXACT IMAGE. AMEN.

CHAPTER 9

IN THE NAME OF JESUS, GOD WITH US

GOD ON THE GROUND

Then the LORD said to Abraham, "Why did Sarah laugh
and say, 'Will I really have a child, now that I am old?'
Is anything too hard for the LORD?"

A frequent question after a disaster is "Where was God when this happened?" When I hear that question, an Old Testament story refreshes my thinking about God's presence.

In the heat of the day, ninety-nine-year-old Abraham sits at the door of his tent, his body digesting his noon meal. In a drowsy stupor, Abraham bobs his head several times before his chin comes to rest on his chest. He looks up to see "three men standing nearby."

Guests! Abraham was delighted when guests arrived, bringing news from far away. He ran from the entrance of his tent to meet them and "bowed low to the ground." He urged the travelers to rest beneath the leafy trees of Mamre and offered water to wash their grimy feet and food for refreshment.

Settling down in the shade, the trio soon dined on Sarah's fresh baked bread, curds, milk, and veal.

On that special day, heavenly guests walked into Abraham and Sarah's lives. Through them God said, "I will return to you at the appointed time next year, and Sarah will have a son." Standing nearby, Sarah overheard God's prophecy and laughed. It seems she added up the contradictions of reality because many years before she and her husband tore down the nursery tent.

Sarah said, "Will I really have a child, now that I am old?" At her age child bearing was impossible. The Lord questioned, "Is anything too hard for the LORD?"

This intimate picture of God seated with Abraham's household scrubs my doubts away and reaffirms to me that God is within my grasp. God came to Abraham's domain, rested in the shade, sat on the ground and ate a meal.

Several things happened when God visited Abraham and Sarah:

> God reaffirmed the earlier promises of an heir.
> God brought truth and clarity to Sarah.
> God conversed and interacted with Abraham and Sarah.
> God made the move to come near to them.
> God initiated changes in their lives.
> God didn't make a big splash when he visited.

This interaction between God and his friends makes me wonder how often I think that God's physical address is heaven? When I have unfulfilled dreams, do I sull up or turn them over to God, believing he is able to make dreams come true according to his will.

Through Abraham's story, I can imagine God as guest, seated on the sofa in my living room, considering my requests. He is near. I can imagine God challenging my unbelief. I will watch for God and dust off the welcome mat, for I long for his nearness, his truth, his clarity.

LORD GOD, ETCH YOUR PROBING QUESTION ONTO MY DREAM-
FILLED HEART: "IS ANYTHING TOO HARD FOR THE LORD?"
IN THE NAME OF JESUS, WHO STILL ABIDES WITH ME.
AMEN.

DISTANCE DINING

Stand at the crossroads and look; ask for the ancient paths,
ask where the good way is, and walk in it.

JEREMIAH 6:16,

A ten-year-old son of a trucker tagged along with his dad to New Mexico to pick up a load of alfalfa from Bill, our farmer friend. While Bill's farm hands loaded the hay, Bill and his foreman Ramón chit-chatted with the boy and learned that this was his first trip to New Mexico. As Bill repeated their conversation to us, he got a big grin on his face.

The boy had looked around at the scenery and told Bill, "I believe I'll walk over to that mountain while the trailer's being loaded."

The foreman Ramón didn't want to discourage him, but knowing the distance and terrain, Ramón asked, "Son, did you bring a lunch? That mountain's a hundred miles away."

We grinned back at Bill when he finished the story. Later that day, I couldn't help thinking about a task looming big in my pathway. God had called me to a quest, but I had set the brake, stopped the forward motion because I felt ill-equipped to tackle the job. Zero confidence. But a reminder from the book of Joshua helped me lay out a plan.

When the Israelites were about to set up residence in the land of Canaan, God delivered a war plan to their leader Joshua. The plan was founded upon God's desire to keep his children from enemy infiltration. God ordained a slaughter to judge generations of evil deeply rooted in Canaan. God wanted to remove the immoral influences from Hebrews' future homeland.

When God issues a difficult calling, he marches before his soldiers, clears a path and even provides daily nourishment. On the battlefields during the wars between Israel and their enemies in Canaan, God was the lead soldier. Prior to one battle and before the hand-to-hand combat started, so much fear formed in the enemies' hearts that they fled into surrounding countries.

At Jericho, God instructed the Hebrews to march around the city 13 times. God then toppled the stone barrier and the Hebrews marched into the heart of Jericho. At other sites, their Chief Commander routed enemies by sending hailstones and lengthening a day.

God is my lead soldier too. When I log in long days and nights living out his calling for my life, God is by my side energizing and directing.

Every time I stare at an unconquerable mountain, I know God will get me around it or over the top. God will clear a path and equip me for the journey. The same God who lengthened a day and changed the weather to aid the Hebrews is beside me.

He has packed my lunch. I can go the distance.

DEAR LORD OF HOSTS, AS YOU JOURNEYED WITH THE HEBREWS, I TRUST YOU TO BE MY LEADER AND REAR GUARD. I LONG FOR YOU TO HIGHLIGHT MY ROAD MAP. KEEP ME ON THE MOST DIRECT ROUTE TO YOU. THROUGH JESUS, THE WAY.
AMEN.

TALKING TO A SHEPHERD

I awoke and looked around. My sleep had been pleasant to me.
JEREMIAH 31:26

Tossing and turning, punching the pillow into a comfortable shape, rearranging night coverings, throwing covers off, getting up to drink water and going back to bed. Those are familiar actions when I am trying to get back to sleep.

Some nights are restless. Sudden wide-eyes and wake-ups can be the result of illness, unsolved problems, spouse's snoring, financial woes, more snoring, concern for loved ones, yet more snoring. Other interruptions are nightmares, unfinished projects, loud noises and guilt. For mature women, decreasing estrogen can cause insomnia.

Medical experts say a newborn needs 18 hours of sleep out of 24, but by the time a child is ten his sleep needs decrease to eight hours. Experts also claim that older adults require less sleep because less energy is expended throughout the day.

Over the years, I've developed a plan for getting back to sleep in the middle of the night. Instead of fussing at my body for waking up, I talk to God and ask for sleep to return. He helps me identify worrisome things on my mind. Sometimes I'm carrying a burden in bed with me. I didn't hand it over to the Father before attempting sleep. Full relinquishment of problems to a loving Father is better than over-the-counter sleep aids.

If sleep doesn't come in five or ten minutes, I then ask God if he awoke me for some particular reason. I recollect that a friend was awakened to discover her clothes dryer extremely overheated after running for four hours while she slept. That wake-up call saved her dryer and may have saved her house.

I've learned it's useless to waste time worrying or counting barnyard animals. I slip out of bed and read the Shepherd's book or talk to the Author, and I express my thanks that "he who watches" over me "will not slumber" (Psalm 121:3b). At other times, I get up and work on quiet projects. When drowsiness recurs, I return to bed.

The non-slumbering God intrigues me. I know God can handle the crazy schedules of earth-occupants, but I cannot imagine finally getting half of the world ready for bed just as the other half is waking up. The Shepherd is equipped for the task, the only one equipped for the 24/7 shift.

I'm relieved God is awake when I can't sleep. I'm ecstatic God isn't a tired, ten-hour shift worker. With gratitude I praise him for his nighttime attention. Many times he has rescued and restored my soul, comforted and made me lie down in green pastures.

NOW I LAY ME DOWN TO SLEEP. I PRAY THEE, LORD,
MY SOUL TO KEEP. IN THE DARKNESS OF NIGHT YOU DO NOT
DOZE; IN THE BRIGHTEST SUNLIGHT YOU NEVER SQUINT.
THANK YOU FOR ALWAYS KEEPING YOUR EYES ON ME.
IN THE NAME OF JESUS, WHO PRAYED THROUGH
THE WATCHES OF THE NIGHT.
AMEN.

LEANING ON JESUS

*Trust in the Lord with all your heart and lean not on your own
understanding; in all your ways acknowledge him and he
will make your paths straight.*

PROVERBS 3:5-6

After a lengthy walk in the country, a weary person looks for a place
to rest such as a fallen tree or a boulder. After a long wait in line at the
drivers license bureau, bank, or grocery store, I find propping against the
counter hard to resist. Fatigued people welcome leaning places.

My husband escorted me to Houston to see Gershwin's musical
"Crazy For You." Near the end of the play, a second drama unfolded next
to us. During a quiet moment of dialogue on stage, an older woman a few
rows over cried out in pain, "Oh, God! Hold me."

Her near seatmates asked if there was a doctor in the house. Others
cried out, "Get an ambulance! Call 9-1-1!" After a few low moans she was
carried out, and ironically, one of the last songs in the musical was "My
Sweet Embraceable You."

Exiting, we saw a group hovering around the woman awaiting medical
attention. We don't know if God allowed her a curtain call or if the
balcony was the final setting for her life, but her words stirred my
imagination. Her words noted an intimacy as she asked God to hold her.
At that moment she needed a leaning place.

Small children who are upset may cry out to their parents, "Hold me."
Caring parents then scoop up their little ones. In need of more than a

quick hug, an exhausted wife may say to her husband, "I just need you to hold me." She will then lean on him and rest in his strength.

God offers himself as a constant leaning place, and Jesus is strong and always available. In the third stanza of E. A. Hoffman's familiar hymn, "Leaning on Jesus," he proclaims, "What have I to fear, leaning on the everlasting arms?"

Today, I noticed how often I rested by shifting my weight to another object. More than once I put my elbows on my desk. Propping my hip against a car fender, I relaxed for a few minutes. Several times I cupped my chin in my palms to relieve the strain in my shoulders. I leaned to ease weariness, remove pressure and to alleviate stress, but my mind and heart needed a leaning place, too.

That kind of rest came when I shifted my load to a bigger shoulder, when I stepped into my Father's embrace and repeated familiar words "Oh, God! Hold me."

ABBA, ABBA, YOU ARE THE ULTIMATE ABIDING PLACE.
MAY YOUR PRESENCE BE AS REAL TO ME AS TO MARY,
WHO SAT AT THE FEET OF JESUS. IN THE NAME OF THE
ONE WHO ALSO INVITED MARTHA TO REST.
AMEN.

GOD AND JONAH

Those who cling to worthless idols forfeit the grace that could be theirs.
But I, with a song of thanksgiving, will sacrifice to you. What I have
vowed I will make good. Salvation comes from the Lord.

JONAH 2:8-9, JONAH'S PRAYER

The story of Jonah is not just a Sunday school lesson for children. In women's Bible class, we found the book of Jonah full of insightful glimpses of God and human nature.

From Jonah's experiences I gained knowledge about God's compassion. In my Bible margins around the Jonah text, I wrote 27 attributes of God. In my heart I added a few more notes of application for me.

Sometimes, God assigns tough tasks, and they are accomplished only when I rely on him. God may design roadblocks when I choose the wrong direction. God provides rescue even during testing. God can woo my heart back toward him, even before my circumstances get better. God extends "second chances" many times. God pursues me as well as the multitude.

From my study I also learned several secular facts. We have firsthand evidence of what happens to people who have been swallowed by large fish. Records of surviving mariners report men with bleached raw skin and the loss of body hair. The stomach acid of a fish is second only to battery acid. Most likely, Jonah was in the same physical condition as modern survivors of such fish capades.

When the fish spit out the reluctant prophet, Jonah finally preached to the Ninevites. "Forty more days and Nineveh will be destroyed," he proclaimed— and the whole city repented. Some estimate the population at 600,000. Most ministers would be elated by such a response. Not Jonah. He became displeased and angry (4:1).

Jonah's passionate prayer expresses his intense displeasure. "That is why I was so quick to flee to Tarshish. I knew that you are a gracious and compassionate God, slow to anger and abounding in Love, a God who relents from sending calamity."

Jonah just wanted to give up, "Now, O LORD, take away my life, for it is better for me to die than to live." Although he knew in his head about God's compassion and loving kindness, his heart was not in sync with God's love for the Ninevites.

Outside of Nineveh, Jonah sulked and waited to see what would happen to thousands of people. God even grew a vine to "give shade for his head and ease his discomfort" (4:6). God "abounding in love" toward Jonah shaded his raw body and his shiny scalp.

God's compassion toward Jonah and the Ninivites caused me to take a look at how I extend mercy. How willing am I to express love when someone rebels from the Father? When I am rejected by acquaintances, am I compassionate? Or do I, like Jonah, sulk under my shade tree, and lick my wounds?

The story of Jonah dramatizes the love of God as he pursues the lost. Jonah and the fish are secondary characters because the real story is about God, who is the Fisher of men.

FATHER, THANK YOU FOR BOLDLY PURSUING ME.
THANK YOU FOR THIS HUGE FISH STORY WHERE YOU NEVER
STRETCHED THE TRUTH. IN THE NAME OF THE ONE WHO
TEACHES ME TO CAST MY NET FOR THE LOST. AMEN.

CHAPTER 10

IN THE NAME OF JESUS COOKING BREAKFAST FOR FRIENDS

Y'ALL COME

They broke bread in their homes and ate together with glad and sincere
hearts, praising God and enjoying the favor of all the people. And the
Lord added to their number daily those who were being saved.

ACTS 2:46-47

"Y'all come." Cline Paden said those were the sweetest words a young
boy could hear. Those words meant the Paden family had an invitation to
dinner after Sunday morning worship.

During the Great Depression food was often scarce, so an invitation to
dine at a neighbor's house signaled a plentiful meal. A growing boy knew
the host's table would most likely be laden with mouth-watering fried
chicken and homegrown vegetables.

Sadly, "Y'all come" is spoken less and less in my busy life. Most
ancestors' food production was labor intensive from seed and stall to
table. My great grandmothers grew their own vegetables, milked cows,
churned butter, baked bread, made jam, and wrung chicken necks.

These chores were part of rearing large families. Yet women still made
time to invite neighbors to "sit a spell." They also took time to prepare a
pot roast and have the visiting preacher over for Sunday dinner.

Desiring to be more hospitable, I planned a luncheon for a few people I
wanted to get to know better. I invited the moms and children to meet me
for an early blueberry picking at a nearby farm. Afterwards, we'd eat a light
lunch at my home. Luncheon day arrived, and the phone began ringing
early. Cancellations poured in from everyone. A sick child. A Saturn slipped

a transmission. Hard candy broke a tooth. Pet cat broke a toenail.

As I walked out the door at 9 a.m. to pick blueberries, my daughter phoned from her workplace to see how preparations were going. I explained my dilemma of too much food and no diners, and she suggested bringing the secretaries in her office for lunch. The "working girls" were delighted by the impromptu invitation to eat homemade chicken salad and fresh blueberry muffins.

Strangers sat down at my table that day, but when the final iced tea was sipped, new friendships had begun. One woman eventually began a Bible study with us and later became a Christian.

Romans 12:13 encourages me to "practice hospitality." The words *hospice, hospital* and *host* embody the idea of treating strangers as guests. Hospitality isn't limited to meals, but the simplest form of entertaining usually does include a meal.

Although modern food conveniences and microwaves have decreased my kitchen workload, I still find issuing meal invitations a challenge. I've yet to serve popcorn as a main course, but I've discovered meal ingredients need not be fancy. In a pinch, I've served takeout food, and even when the house was a bit mussed, guests didn't seem to mind folding the laundry while I diced potatoes for the soup.

My goal is to host more strangers, to practice hospitality, to phone more neighbors and say, "Y'all come."

FATHER, THANK YOU FOR PRESERVING IN SCRIPTURE THE
INTIMATE DINING SCENES OF JESUS AND HIS DISCIPLES,
EXACT IMAGES OF YOUR CARE. IN THE NAME OF THE SEASHORE
JESUS, WHO KEPT FOOD WARM OVER BURNING COALS
AND WAITED FOR HIS FRIENDS. AMEN.

OATMEAL DAYS

*For I have chosen him, so that he will direct his children
and his household after him to keep the way of the Lord by doing
what is right and just . . . .*

GENESIS 18:19, GOD SPEAKING ABOUT ABRAHAM

Oatmeal days. Not days like graduation days, wedding days or birthing days. Ordinary days. Days when nothing special is going on. Such plain days are for vacuuming, making Jell-O, matching socks and paying bills. These are the days commonly on my mind.

In connection with common days, I've especially been thinking about the patriarch Abraham. On such plain days, Abraham was probably making sure his huge tribe had food, clothing and shelter. Besides superintending his family, the Genesis text mentions 318 trained men born in his household who helped protect his nomadic compound. He fed an army! Abraham had plenty of common days filled with everyday chores: overseeing his possessions and herdsmen, eating, sleeping, enjoying his family, traveling, taking naps on rainy days, training his army, inspecting fabric for new tents, trading choice flock for food and delicacies.

Abraham's ordinary days must have far outnumbered his glory days. He lived 63,875 days to the age of 175. In his biblical biography, there are approximately 27 milestone events recorded. If each distinct event took one year to unfold, Abraham might have used up 27 years of his life span for special days. I suspect those leftover 148 years brought a lot of ordinary days.

Oatmeal days is a coined phrase one woman attaches to no-frill-or-thrill days. God assigns oatmeal days to each family unit, and the plentiful, plain days offer many times to direct family to follow the ways of the Lord.

Sometimes guilt attacks like a hornet when I'm involved in mundane chores like scrubbing floors or sweeping down cobwebs from my back porch. When that happens, I've deemed those tasks not as valuable in the sight of God as spooning soup into an invalid's mouth, but every act of service is important to living out God's purpose.

Whether my days are "oatmeal ordinary" or "Richter-scale grand," each day is an opportunity for obeying God's assignment. On ho-hum days when my family tract is kept tidy and functional, it is being readied so those in my care can "keep the way of the Lord, by doing what is just and right" (Genesis 18:19).

LORD OF ALL MY DAYS, EVEN MY DUSTING AND MOPPING, LEAD ME TO 100 PER CENT DEVOTION. IN THE NAME OF JESUS, WHO TOLD A KINGDOM STORY ABOUT A WOMAN SWEEPING A HOUSE. AMEN.

TURTLES IN TIGHT SPOTS

But I, by your great mercy, will come into your house; in reverence
will I bow down toward your holy temple. Lead me, O LORD,
in your righteousness because of my enemies—
make straight your way before me.

PSALM 5:7-8

One spring I walked the perimeter of our yard picking up debris from a windstorm. Ducking under low cedar limbs, I discovered a turtle shell. There is no way of knowing the full story of the turtle's death, but I discovered a few facts.

One side of our country yard is fenced by medium gauge wire, shaped into square openings six by seven inches. The turtle's shell had firmly wedged in the middle of one of these rectangles, and no pertinent remains remained. I cringed at first sight of it. How long had he struggled to get free? Do turtles have voices? If he'd cried out, would we have heard him?

Traveling to his destination, the turtle obviously made an error in judgment. Perhaps he wrongly assumed he could squeeze through a tight spot and still make his goal. Maybe he absentmindedly struggled forward in spite of obvious pressure, when he should have backed off and tried another route. Perhaps his insensitive shell was unable to "feel" as the wires ensnared him and became his final prison.

Robert Lamont tells another turtle story from his childhood. "When I was a school boy we would occasionally see a turtle on a fence post and when we did, we knew someone had put him there. He didn't get there by himself."

The turtles in both stories were stranded, but there is a vast difference in the dilemmas of the turtle trying to travel through my yard and the turtle in Dr. Lamont's story. My turtle walked into the predicament; the others were waylaid by outside forces.

The pitiable turtle stories made me think of my Christian walk. Some mornings I plunge into tasks without prayer for the work at hand. Before realizing it, I have straggled until noon and accomplished nothing substantial. On other mornings, unexpected schedule changes tangle my plans, and I am tempted to whine. However, when I remember to emulate my brother, King David, I don't get wedged in fences or fret when I have to sit on a fence post.

David's words have become one of my prayer favors asked of God. "Morning by morning, O LORD, you hear my voice; morning by morning I lay my requests before you and wait in expectation..." (5:3).

What a difference a prayer makes. James's words also speak truth to me about the outcome of my days. "You do not have, because you do not ask God" (3:2). Dawn by dawn, I try to start my mornings with God because there might be a "tight spot" ahead in my day, and I don't want to stick my neck out without a blessing.

FATHER, TOO MANY DAYS, I HIT THE FLOOR RUNNING.
HELP ME TO RUN TO YOU. IN THE NAME OF JESUS, WHO SAID YOU
SEE INTO MY PRAYER CLOSET AND MEET ME THERE.
AMEN.

FRIENDSHIP

A friend loveth at all times.

PROVERBS 17:17

An elderly friend made a generous offer to my family. Her prolific fall garden produced a crop of turnip greens, our favorite vegetable. "Come pick anytime" was Connie's kind invitation, but her turnip greens matured the exact week of a large family wedding.

Out-of-towners arrived expecting Tex-Mex dishes. Tuxedos needed to be picked up, and beds needed clean linens. Disappointed, I turned down Connie's generous offer.

Greens require a lot of "attention" before the first fork full is ever enjoyed. The majority of work is in the de-sanding process. Large leafed greens require several hosings outside, a few kitchen sink washings, then several rounds of draining and inspections to assure all sand is rinsed away. For the delicate palate, grit and greens don't mix.

After greens are clean, they get the boiling water plunge, minimizing fluffiness. Next, they are cooled in ice water and drained before freezing. The entire process, called blanching, leaves the vitamins intact. The grit's gone. The good stuff is saved.

During the busy wedding week, I phoned my friend Doris. I learned she'd received the same offer from Connie. We discussed a rather unusual, but perhaps easier method of ridding greens of sand with the aid of a washing machine. After our telephone conversation, my mind was back on bows and beaus and bells and belles. I forgot about gleaning greens.

After the wedding, exhaustion set in, but within a few days my husband and I were sitting up again and taking nourishment. That's when my friend Doris phoned and asked if she could drop by. In half an hour, she knocked on our back door. When I answered her knock, I saw an ice chest, a huge blue bowl and a meek smile on her face. She brought 15 bags of frozen greens and a bowl of bacon-flavored cooked greens.

Truth is—back door guests are best. Doris picked greens, used the washing machine technique and froze greens for our family. Again, her Southern hospitality showed. For over 30 years, Doris has made an imprint on my heart through her around-the-clock friendship.

In my relationship with friends, whether I share tea and crumpets or tears and tissues, I need to remember the lesson from the greens.

Keep washing away the grit. Save the good stuff.

DEAR GOD, I LIFT MY HANDS IN THANKSGIVING FOR MY DEVOTED FRIENDS. I LIFT UP THOSE WHO STICK BY MY SIDE THROUGH CELEBRATIONS AND DO NOT ABANDON ME IN NEEDY, DARKER MOMENTS. IN THE NAME OF MY BEST FRIEND, JESUS. AMEN.

CHAPTER 11

IN THE NAME OF JESUS HEALING LONGTIME CRIPPLES

ONE MORE NIGHT WITH FROGS

. . . let us purify ourselves from everything that contaminates body and spirit, perfecting holiness out of reverence for God.

2 CORINTHIANS 7:1-2

The frogs crept up from the Nile and entered the palace of the king. The warty things wallowed in his bed and bread bowls; they even sheltered in the cool ovens. Chairs and floors were upholstered in green, and with their sticky feet they clung to people and walls. God brought the plague of frogs on the Egyptians as part of a plan to rescue the enslaved Hebrews and to gain glory for God. Those frogs remind me of sin.

Like frogs, sins creep in and cling. Some offenders try to hide their sins from spouse, coworkers, children, community, or church. Hidden indiscretions range from cheating on income taxes to cheating in marriage, from stealing pencils to embezzling, from slothful parenting to abuse, from neglect of others to indulgence of self. Camouflage is clothing, but not the way of a godly life.

Secret sin rarely stays silent; it has a way of hopping to headline news. Any sin produces rotten fruit, and contamination starts to show up in the life of the perpetrator. Sins seem to have their own pride, and sooner or later they boast or leave telltale signs in their host. The only place for wrongs is in the healing hand of God.

Back in Egypt, God's servant Moses helped in the frog extermination and said to Pharaoh, "I leave to you the honor of setting the time for me to pray for you and your officials and your people that you and your houses may be rid of the frogs" (Exodus 8:9).

What would my answer have been? "Yesterday. This instant. Right now. Just get the slimy green things out of my sight and off my pillows."

Pharaoh answered, "Tomorrow." Perhaps he answered "Tomorrow" because ancient Egyptians deified frogs, but for some reason he wanted to spend one more night with the croaking amphibians.

Some of my sins have been with me for many nights. When my wrong doings don't cause me much misery, then I may delight in them a little longer. An example of my sin is overeating. If I'm not gaining weight or suffering too much heartburn, I continue to overeat, and like Pharaoh and the frogs, I want to spend one more night with my "cherished" sin.

Paul preached purity, meaning decontamination of body and spirit. For me, purity means checking the secret chambers of my heart and remembering the frogs. I don't want to spend another night with them.

GOD, I REPEAT DAVID'S PLEA, "FORGIVE MY HIDDEN FAULTS." BRING INTO THE OPEN ANY SINS LURKING IN THE CORNERS OF MY HEART. IN THE NAME OF JESUS, WHO SHINES ON ME. AMEN.

DIRT SHOWER

Do not take revenge, my friends, but leave room for God's wrath,
for it is written: "It is mine to avenge; I will repay," says the Lord.

ROMANS 12:19

A steamy shower and a comfortable place to pillow my head when I'm tired are my favorite creature comforts. Each day the luxury of warm, cascading water rinses off the grime of work and refreshes me. But another kind of shower occasionally comes my way.

The dirt shower.

Dirt and words were slung at the barefoot King David fleeing Jerusalem with his entourage of thousands. David's son Absalom had challenged his father's ability to govern. The story unfolds in 2 Samuel 15 and 16 when Absalom established himself as king in Hebron and set his sight on the Jerusalem throne. The next events in David's story are not a surprise because "when it rains it pours."

David faced more trouble as another enemy attacked. Shimei, from King Saul's family, confronted King David as they approached Bahurim and cursed him. David's loyal subjects wanted to run Shimei off or, more accurately, run him through. The servant Abishai specifically suggested, "Let me go over and cut off his head" (16:9).

David persuaded his protectors that this assault was to be endured and lessons learned. Shimei continued pelting David, his officials, troops and special guards. Trotting alongside the travelers, Shimei slung stones and curses and showered his enemy with dirt. Finally, Shimei quit. Later, the "king and all the people with him arrived at their destination." Exhausted, David refreshed himself (16:14).

King David said to those who would kill Shimei, "If he is cursing because the Lord said to him 'Curse David,' who can ask, 'Why do you do this?'" David also said, "It may be that the Lord will repay me with good for the cursing I am receiving today" (16:10-12).

King David chose to look above the head of his accuser to the judgment seat of God. The king reasoned that evil often confronts God's children and the circumstances can become an avenue of self-examination. David also chose to believe God could bring good out of a destructive situation.

I know what it feels like to get a dirt shower, and I can empathize with David. Oh, how I prefer the days when I receive compliments. On those days it's easy to stay upbeat and worry-free. But how do I react when someone chooses to berate me when I'm hanging on by spider silk? How do I react when criticism is drenching me?

Dirt showers are inevitable for Christ followers. When they come, the Father expects me to respond like my brother Jesus. He doesn't want me to join in mudslinging. He wants me to rise above it.

FATHER, HELP ME TO RESIST GOSSIP, SQUABBLES AND IMMEDIATE
RETALIATION. GIVE ME PATIENCE TO WAIT FOR YOU TO LEVEL
MY PATH. I ASK IN THE NAME OF MY SAVIOR, WHO
STOOD MUTE BEFORE HIS ACCUSERS.
AMEN.

FAITH AND FULL

We live by faith, not by sight.

2 CORINTHIANS 5:7

At age four, our daughter Sheryle loved to play a game she invented. Approaching her dad or me she would say, "Close your eyes and open your mouth." Trusting my preschooler to drop something edible into my mouth was a test of my faith.

We usually shook our heads and said, "No."

Undaunted, she begged and pleaded, "Trust me!" Finally, we would shut our eyes and open our mouths. Immediately, some morsel—an M&M, popcorn or other tiny treat—delighted our taste buds.

I must confess my fears ran rampant when she entered a room, hands behind her back and uttered, "Close your eyes and open your mouth." Sheryle never disappointed us. She proved trustworthy, and no grasshoppers or dust bunnies were ever placed on our tongues.

When God rescued Israel from Egyptian slavery, he challenged them to trust him. Bringing thousands upon thousands of Hebrews into a desert, he asked them to look to him for their daily needs.

How difficult it must have been to put little ones to bed in the wilderness, knowing there wasn't enough food to feed thousands of growling stomachs. But one morning with the dew, the master of surprise rained down manna, a resin-looking food substance.

"What is it?" the Hebrews asked when they saw the white matter lying on the ground. Their question became the identifying name for the substance. For forty years Israel ate "What is it?"

God had a few rules about manna: the people were to gather it each morning and not save any until the next day. The day before the Sabbath, they were to gather enough for two days. Had I been one of those nomadic women, I probably would have failed this faith test. What breadless woman throws out leftovers in the desert?

God told his people to throw out leftovers, pillow their heads without anxiety, and fully trust him as their provider. Some did. Some did not.

Often I find myself in the camp with the some-did-not. Because of my stubborn nature, it is difficult for me to fully believe that God keeps his promises. The Hebrews needed more faith lessons too, and they were in the wilderness classroom for forty years.

God's words about this part of Israel's history are recorded in Psalm 81: "I am the Lord your God, who brought you up out of Egypt. Open wide your mouth and I will fill it." Along with this command, he offered a promise: "If my people would but listen to me, if Israel would follow my ways, how quickly would I subdue your enemies... you would be fed with the finest wheat; with honey from the rock I would satisfy you" (10-16).

Like the Hebrews, I need faith-building circumstances. "Open wide your mouth" isn't a game with God. Even today, it's God's plan for increasing my faith, for subduing my enemies, for feeding me the "finest wheat" and "honey from the rock."

LORD GOD, PROVIDER, LEAD ME TO THE BREAD OF LIFE,
LEAD ME NOT INTO THE WILDERNESS OF WANDERING.
IN THE PRECIOUS NAME OF JESUS, WHO AUTHORS AND
FINISHES MY FAITH. AMEN

SATAN'S SCHEMES

*Your enemy the devil prowls around like a roaring lion looking for
someone to devour. Resist him, standing firm in the faith . . .*

1 PETER 5:8

I am persuaded that during the time Jesus walked on earth, Satan
stalked and roared overtime. My persuasion comes from the gospel
accounts of the many distractions placed in Jesus' path. Yet Jesus
remained steadfast and on mission his entire life. My direction in life
can be easily sidetracked, too, by God's archenemy.

Sometimes when Jesus healed people, he sent them away with a
thanksgiving instruction. On one occasion when he healed a man of
leprosy, he said: "See that you don't tell this to anyone... Instead he (the
healed leper) went out and began to talk freely... as a result Jesus could no
longer enter a town openly" (Mark 1:43-45). This healed man didn't obey
Jesus, so Jesus instantly became a local celebrity, consistently surrounded
by a crowd of people. At least 42 times, Matthew makes mention of the
crowds that encompassed Jesus.

Of course Jesus loved all people, but he also needed an allotment of
unencumbered time to accomplish spiritual grooming of the disciples.
Mark 9:30 says, "Jesus did not want anyone to know where they were,
because he was teaching his disciples." He also needed personal solitude
for meditation and time with the Father to seek his counsel.

Sandwiched between Mark's account of the two miracles in which
Christ feeds the 5,000 and walks on water, two transitional sentences tell

me a lot about the Christ: "Immediately Jesus made his disciples get into the boat and go on ahead of him to Bethsaida, while he dismissed the crowd. After leaving them, he went into the hills to pray" (Mark 6:45-46).

The words indicate that Jesus took control of his life. He triumphed by sticking with God's agenda. Note his actions. He "made his disciples get into the boat." He "dismissed the crowd," and "leaving them, he went into the hills to pray."

Often my days are "crowded" by time wasters, selfish entertainment, and yes, too many people sometimes. Satan is up to his old tricks. He's sneaky. When my eyes wander from God's calling, I'm more easily snared by devilish allurements. Satan is flashy. He's sneaky and cunning. He roars up on a Harley and I jump into the sidecar for the worst rides of my life.

Through Mark's words, Jesus provides an aggressive pattern to follow. He encourages me to place limitations on activities that drain my walk with God. Willard Tate wrote, "One day, I believe, we'll either rejoice over what we did with our lives with God's help, or else we'll weep secretly over what we let life do to us."

FATHER, YOUR ENEMY AND MINE, THAT DEVIL, KEEPS MAKING
APPEARANCES. WHEN HE KNOCKS, HELP ME REMEMBER
TO ASK JESUS, "WILL YOU GET THAT DOOR."
AMEN.

THE GRACE SHAKER

Be wise in the way you act toward outsiders; make the most of every
opportunity. Let your conversation be always full of grace, seasoned
with salt, so that you may know how to answer everyone.

COLOSSIANS 4:5-6

Corn chowder bubbles on the range. Cornbread browns in the oven, and the Caesar salad is chilling in the refrigerator. The last chore before dinner is the taste test. Blowing steam away from the hot liquid in the spoon, I taste the broth. Bland. The soup needs salt.

In my years of homemaking, I have over-seasoned food many times. On other days, the food I served was monotonous, offered straight from a can without much thought for those who slid their feet under my table.

Although those meals eased my family's hunger pangs, they were not mouth-watering good. On the other hand, a recipe prepared with care brought acclamations from the diners. I want to season my words in the same appetizing way.

"Bite your tongue" is an old phrase that means to stop speaking what you are saying. How many times did I hear my parents say, "If you can't say something nice, don't say anything"? As a parent I often offered the same ultimatum of speaking kind words or remaining quiet.

A rewind button on a tongue could be a help. Many times I've wished a word, intonation, or a whole conversation could be deleted. Working on a plan to help me speak more pleasing words, I began with a castaway salt shaker.

My salt shaker is one of a set. It consists of a man and a woman, each with two faces. On one side of the shakers, the man and woman wear scowls. On the other side their faces sport jolly smiles.

On a piece of small paper I wrote GRACE in bold letters. I taped the paper around the base of the female salt shaker, on her smiley face side, and placed it alongside my kitchen range. The GRACE shaker became a visual reminder to season my conversations with good-natured words.

I also wrote Colossians 4:5-6 on an index card and taped it to my computer desk. Last, I memorized the two verses from Colossians because I need the season-conversations-with-grace scripture in my heart.

"Taste and see that the LORD is good" (Psalm 34:8) is an invitation for people to experience God's bounty from food to mercy. In conversations, I make God palatable or distasteful, and the GRACE shaker and scriptures remind me to make the most of every opportunity, to sprinkle grace conversationally.

LORD GOD, I DISH OUT A LOT OF WORDS THAT SHOULD NEVER BE SPOONED UP ON SOMEONE ELSE'S PLATE. ABRIDGE MY MOUTH. GIVE ME A DICTIONARY FULL OF GRACIOUS WORDS. IN THE NAME OF THE TEMPLE CLEANSER.

AMEN.

CHAPTER 12

IN THE NAME OF JESUS, CHRIST IN ME

A KING IN A TENT

The Word became flesh and lived for awhile among us.
We have seen his glory, the glory of the one and only Son,
who came from the Father, full of grace and truth.

JOHN 1:14

"God Pitches a Tent" is the title of my favorite chapter in *Was Christ God?* by Spiros Zodhiates. My camping experiences, especially assembling tents, gives me better understanding of Logos, the Word, coming to earth. Immanuel, God with us, lived in the makeshift shelter of a human body.

Zodhiates' entire book is an exposition of John 1:1-18. Several chapters are devoted to one verse. "The word became flesh and lived for awhile among us" (John 1:14). The verb "lived" is translated from a Greek word that means "tented." At just the right time in the history of mankind, the Christ, God robed in flesh, camped on the earth in a tent body.

The flesh-body is also compared to a temple, a tabernacle, a tent for God's spirit (1 Corinthians 6:19). Several thousand years ago, God fashioned a tiny infant tabernacle, and Jesus entered the world through the womb of a woman.

When the astrologers during the days of Daniel said gods "do not live among men" (2:11), they were right. Their stone and wooden images held no hope of a heartbeat, and their pagan idols possessed no helping hand or sympathetic tear. On the other hand, YAWEH desired that all humankind receive an accurate image of the true, invisible God (Colossians 1:15), because he is the living God that does dwell with men.

On a long ago night outside of Bethlehem, there were shepherds living in the fields and tending their flocks. An angel entered this pastoral scene bringing good news."This will be a sign to you: You will find a baby wrapped in strips of cloth and lying in a manger" (Luke 2:12).

The shepherds marveled at the magnitude of the message. Perhaps they understood that the baby they went to see wasn't only given to Joseph and Mary. The birth-announcement angel had said: "I bring you good news of great joy that will be for all the people. Today in the town of David a Savior has been born to you; he is Christ the Lord" (2:10-11).

Has the wonder of my Savior arriving in flesh been lost to me? If so, I will journey to the field and listen to the angel speak. I will walk into Bethlehem with the inquiring shepherds and search the side streets looking for the newborn child. Then I will rediscover the amazing truth that God is both giver and gift.

Those sheep-tenders heard the universal message, and they reacted in a personal way. Luke said, "When they had seen him, they spread the word concerning what had been told them about this child . . . " (2:17).

The King of Kings pitched a tent in enemy territory and experienced all my battles and joys. He yearns to be in my heart, on my mind and wrapped around my soul. Years ago, he knocked on the canvas door of my heart, and I invited him in.

He made himself at home because my God has lived in a tent before.

HOLY GOD, I MARVEL THAT THE LIKES OF YOU KEEPS COMPANY WITH ME. I CAN ONLY SAY THANK YOU IN HUMILITY. MAY I, LIKE THE SHEPHERDS, "SPREAD THE WORD" ABOUT THE SAVIOR. IN THE NAME OF JESUS, WHO CAMPED HERE WITH US. AMEN.

WHEN I SEE A CROSS

Carrying his own cross, he went out to The Place of the Skull....

JOHN 19:17

An early-rising rooster awakened my husband and me at a bed and breakfast in Cat Spring, Texas. Longhorn cattle, horses and a braying donkey also shared the country estate. We lodged in a converted Dutch barn suite with a fireplace. In a tree near our private porch, a caged dove cooed softly through the temperature-perfect get-away weekend.

One afternoon of our stay, I rested on a day bed near an open window and noticed a small stained glass cross dangling by a delicate thread and bobbling in the breeze. Later that day on the B & B grounds, we toured a larger cabin under construction. The open concept structure had two levels, lower and loft. Near a skylight in an exposed gable, I spied a vivid crimson glass cross.

Curious about the crosses, I asked our hostess, Sunny, why she displayed crosses in her guestrooms. Her answer was simple. She wanted her guests to "remember where they came from, what they're doing here, and where they're going."

Later, I wrote the date of our visit and Sunny's words in the margin of my Bible where John recorded a similar statement about Jesus and the last supper with his disciples. I love the phraseology of John's words: "Jesus knew... that he had come from God and was returning to God" (13:3).

John also recorded that Jesus "got up from the meal, took off his outer clothing, and wrapped a towel around his waist" before he "poured water into a basin..." to use for washing his disciples' feet. Afterwards, he dried their feet "with the towel that was wrapped around him" (13:4-5).

On this night before his cross, Jesus showed his disciples the full extent of the Father's love. His love expression is an example to me about how I am to serve others in the remaining years before my death. Jesus lived the middle part, the what-I-am-doing-here years, in a stunning manner.

Ever since our visit to Cat Spring, I am more aware of crosses. They are everywhere. A framed, tatted cross is on my computer desk. Another cross marks a fatality site between my property and my neighbor's. Jewelers fashion crosses, studding some with precious jewels. They dangle from earlobes and grace necks. Steeples and graves are ornamented by this historic symbol.

Crosses are a common sight, and I want them to remind me of Jesus' mid-life, the years between birth and death. When I see a cross, I want to remember the Servant.

I want to remember why I'm here.

LORD JESUS, IT'S TOO EASY FOR MY EYES TO SKIM OVER THIS
SYMBOL BECAUSE I AM CENTURIES REMOVED FROM ITS TERROR.
I AM ASHAMED TO SAY THAT TO YOU. PLEASE, WHENEVER
I SEE A CROSS, REMIND ME, LAMB OF GOD, YOU WERE
A DAILY LIVING SACRIFICE TOO.
AMEN.

THE POWER TO GIVE

Whoever wishes to be great among you must be your servant... just as the
Son of Man came not to be served, but to serve.

MATTHEW 20:26-28

A peasant woman walked many miles to visit a female missionary and bring a gift. The appreciative receiver genuinely was uneasy about the length of the giver's journey and expressed her concern. The giver's reply was classic, "The journey is part of the gift."

The power to give in a selfless way comes from above. When giving comes to mind, too often I think of trinkets, cards, and gift wrap. Or I think of money dropped into a polished aluminum plate on Sundays. All are legitimate gifts, but what about the journey? If my bank account is substantial, even a generous monetary gift will "cost" me very little.

What would I do if someone approached me with this arrangement: "I will teach you how to give. First, you must let go of everything you own and start out empty handed." I would consider the proposition for quite some time before accepting or not.

Lately when reading the gospels and Philippians 2, I've been most impressed by what Jesus gave up to live here on earth. He willingly gave up his place with God and surrounded himself with people like me. His humble journey to earth was part of his gift.

What other gifts did he bring to his earthly companions? He shared very few material possessions. Jesus said to those who inquired about joining his troupe, "Foxes have holes and birds of the air have nests, but the Son of Man has no place to lay his head (Luke 9:58). Jesus may not have had a pillow or a place to cradle his head, but he was able to assist the homeless with a good night's sleep because he knew the secret of giving.

Jesus knows humanity yearns for lasting things. Coins only take up temporary residence in pockets, and the glitz of gifts soon fades. Jesus knew what to give. He gave himself. He taught. He healed. He touched. He laughed. He brought God into people's lives. Every day he put personal desires aside to assist others. Jesus' sacrifice wasn't only at the end of his life, it was daily.

On my journey, I haven't learned to fully give of my time and abilities like Jesus, but I want to. I haven't laid aside all my selfish desires, but I want to. Too often I approach the needy with a gift bag in my hand. When I give only a token gift, something is missing. I know "who" is missing. Jesus is missing, the spirit of Jesus.

In *The God of the Towel*, Jim McGuiggan explains how Jesus was able to continually give for others' benefit. "The Father gave [Jesus] all power, because every time he gave him some, he used it to bless others." When my heart finally has one Master, he will be the keeper of my front and back doors. Only then will God's love flow continually through my temporary dwelling to assist and truly love others.

That's when my journey becomes part of my gift.

GOD OF MY WALK THROUGH LIFE, FILL MY HEART WITH JESUS.
ONLY THEN WILL I BE EQUIPPED WITH POWER TO GIVE LIKE YOU.
PLEASE, SHINE THROUGH ME LORD. IN THE NAME OF JESUS,
THE LIGHT OF THE WORLD.
AMEN.

THREE COATS

...we will tell the next generation the praiseworthy deeds of the LORD,
his power, and the wonders he has done.

PSALM 78:4B

In three closets, in three different houses hang three family members' coats. They are tattered work garments, each symbolizing a son's love and loyalty in three stories of father-son relationships. The men who own and wear the coats are Harold, David and Russell and are grandfather, son and grandson.

One Christmas season, the grandson Russell, living on the family farm, noticed his grandpa Harold's work coat was rather frayed and worn. As a demonstration of his love and gratitude, Russell went shopping and purchased a top-of-the-line work coat for a Christmas gift.

A few days before December 25th, Harold was as usual wearing his old familiar coat while haying the cows. When the feeding was finished, Russell asked his grandpa to come into his house to open an early present. Eagerly, Harold ripped off the wrapping paper, lifted the box lid, pulled back the tissue and uncovered a heavy duty work coat.

Russell said, "I thought you needed a new one. That old one's so ragged."

Harold told his grandson, "This is my daddy's coat." Immediately, Russell understood that his grandpa had kept and worn his father's old coat as a reminder of his dad who died in 1948 when Harold was only 28 years old. On frosty mornings for 50 years, Harold faithfully slipped his arms into his dad's jacket. His dad was a model, dependable family man.

The men in my family discovered they all had something in common. Harold wore his dad's coat for 50 years. Harold's son David has his father's navy coat from World War II and has worn it most winters since his teenage years. The grandson Russell also wears his daddy's army jacket from his military service in Vietnam.

These fathers passed on more than denim blue and olive green jackets. The jackets of the older generations are trophies displaying their fathers' faith in country, family and God. The cultivated values the jackets represent are evidence that the roots in the past now thread through four generations. In this age of great challenges, the younger generations are able to reflect on the heritage of courage and honorable labor, a backdrop to which they can look and find a standard for living.

Elbow grease, chores and wars have taxed the fabrics. Though the coats are frayed and worn, my family continues to preserve them. They will not be sold in a yard sale. The jackets will not be tossed out. On chilly days, they do more than provide warmth to men's bodies. They symbolize a godly heritage that warms my family's soul.

FATHER, I THANK YOU FOR PAST GENERATIONS WHO LOVED YOU AND PRESENT FAMILY MEMBERS WHO ADORE YOU. FOR FUTURE GENERATIONS, MAY THEY HEAR YOUR WORD AND OBEY. PLEASE CARRY ON YOUR GOOD NAME IN MY FAMILY. IN THE NAME OF JESUS, AN HONORABLE SON TO JOSEPH, MARY AND YOU. AMEN.